Six Brief Memoirs
David Macpherson

Introduction

Six pieces of my life. Small things. Slivers.

People ask how long it takes to write a book. This can be a difficult question. It is not easy to know when you started something and some writers are never sure when it is done.

With this book, I know exactly how long it took me to write this. Eighteen days.

I spent three days for each of these little memoirs. That's it.

From March 2020 to March 2021, I put out 13 issues of an eZine. The first three issues had the ridiculous name The Hangover Hour Report. After the third issue, I realized my wicked ways and changed it to The Long Weekend Review.

The hook for all the issues of this zine is that they could be whatever the writer wanted to create, as long as the work was done in three days.

I'm a big fan of immediacy and this was a terrific way to create something without any second guessing or nail biting. You didn't have time to worry, you had a small book to write.

The first issue was a list of things to do while we are in lockdown due to pandemic. The second one was a story by the writer Jeff Campbell.

For the third issue, I decided to write an issue. I think I saw a version of the Rocky Horror Show on YouTube and figured I would write a memoir in three days about everything I remember about being a kid going to Rocky Horror every weekend. I called it, My Life in the Frank-N-Furter Cult and it might be my favorite writing experience.

In three days, I wrote something that I was not intending to be so personal. It turned into a piece I was not expecting and I loved the experience. I wanted others to do this and I got 4 memoirs written in three days by other writers.

Throughout that year, I filled in the gaps of the monthly schedule by writing my own three days books. Most of them were memoirs, because it was so much fun.

I wrote six of these three day memoirs in the course of the year. The last one tells the story of that year and how I set about writing them, so I don't think I need to rehash that here.

Just to say that I think that writing a memoir is three days is the perfect length for such a thing. It gets to the heart of the tale you want to tell.

Some of them are things I am quite proud of. One or two of these memoirs don't seem to work as well. I won't tell you which, I will let you discover those. But with one, I was trying to do something different, and I don't think I succeeded. With that said, I am not holding back any of this work. Let it stand or fall on your judgement.

This book contains eighteen days of writing that took a lifetime to prepare for.

Thank you for reading.

David

My Life in the Frank-N-Furter Cult

Begun 10 am, April 20th, 2020.

1

Everyone plays with their number. No one is accurate when they are asked what their number is. How old are you? How many partners have you had? How many hours did you study for this test?

How many times have we fancied up the total? We think the real number is never as good for our image as one we can fabricate. 50 becomes 41 becomes 39. 4 becomes 7 becomes 11 becomes so many I can't remember. Numbers are flexible.

Numbers make us seem more dedicated. Numbers give you an impression of how cool, how mad, how focused we are. Got to have the right number for the person we want to be.

D'Isreali said there are three kinds of lies: lies, damned lies, and statistics. Numbers are not to be trusted. Hell, this quote can't be trusted. D'Istreali probably wasn't the one to say it. It doesn't mean that it isn't true. It doesn't mean that numbers lie all the time. Who's D'Isreali anyway? What role did he play in the floor show?

When I tell about my time with Rocky Horror, I am aware of the lies and exaggerations. I have lied about my amount of participation. About how much it means to me in my life. But there is nothing that Rocky Horror people lie about more than their number.

How many times have you gone to Rocky Horror Picture Show?

This was a big deal. People would make announcements of their anniversaries. "This is Kendra's 100th showing of Rocky Horror." And everyone clapped and cheered and wondered when they would get to 100 showings and imagine the applause they would receive. For what? For seeing a movie a lot of times?

There was a guy who was part of the front row crowd when we went to Rocky Horror at Pearl River Theater. He hung out with us seventeen year old kids but he was older. He was well into his twenties. He didn't have most of his teeth. He smelled of dirty clothes and old cigarettes. He was loud and pushy, so he kind of ran the front row.

I noticed he was off a lot with his numbers. In the summer of 1986 he had at least three anniversaries. In the beginning he told us this was 100th showing of Rocky. Somewhere in August, he was at 150 viewings. Then, when I got back from school in October, he was at his 200th. The movie played only twice a week. Midnight on Friday and Saturdays. The math didn't work.

But who gives a fuck about the math? He told us his number and we believed it. We cheered. We were in awe at his dedication. He was making it work. He was annoying and I didn't like him, but I still wished I could be that important to the Rocky scene.

I spent a lot of my time trying to keep my number straight. For a hot second, I even wrote down the dates of my attendance in a notebook dedicated solely to this endeavor. That didn't last. It became one of those wasted notebooks that only had one or two pages written on. The rest of the pages were blank. So much unrecorded history. I wasn't good at tracking my homework and my friend's phone numbers. There was not a chance in hell I was going to preserve my life with Rocky Horror.

Even this. This is just a gaze backwards through a lot of mist and blackout pauses.

If you pressed me, and I rather you didn't, I will say that i have seen The Rocky Horror Picture Show about fifty times. When I say that, watching it on video doesn't count. For this to count, it must be in a theater with people shouting at the screen. Of course, there are people throwing toast and firing off water guns. There were people dressed up in costume too, but I wasn't sure how I felt about that.

No. For me, Rocky Horror was all about shouting and acting out with the screen Going up at the end of the movie and pretending to spin the movie image and that spun into the globe on the Criminologist's desk. That was one of my favorite things in the world to do. Better yet, was shouting a line at the screen by myself, not in chorus with others, and getting a laugh. Like I created that line. Like I deserve the title of Artist just for the act of reciting a line well. That was Rocky Horror for me.

I saw it 50 times. Or maybe it was 62. Maybe it was 37. I was drunk some of the time. I was tired all of the time. How could anyone be expected to recall. But there have been times when I have told people, "Yeah. I was a big Rocky kid. I went every weekend." Not true. "I was part of the floor show." Just twice. And I was awful. "I went something like 100, 150 times."

Who was I trying to impress? The people I was talking to? They didn't care. Myself? Probably. How could I be allowed to go on and on about Rocky if I was just a midnight movie tourist? How can I write a whole book (albeit a short one) about my time with Rocky if I am just a low numbered wannabe?

And yet. Here we are. With my forgotten number and my spotty memory. I will flashback to things I might not recall or understand. I will discover things like it was new. Like it always was when returning from another era. I will do the Time Warp, again.

2

I learned about The Rocky Horror Picture Show from Tom Bosley. Yeah. The guy who played the dad in Happy Days. He introduced me to this world.

He was the narrator of a syndicated TV show about movies and show biz called "That's Hollywood." My family watched it every week. In my small family, we had certain shows we watched every week together. There was Sha-Na-Na, Wild Kingdom, reruns of Soap and the Carol Burnett Show. And That's Hollywood was one of the ones we all watched together. I think that was because I was such a movie freak.

Each episode was focused on a theme. There were episodes on classics, on science fiction movies, and so on. Then there was on a midnight movies. They featured the Rocky Horror Picture Show. There was the wholesome, reedy voice of Tom Bosley talking about the Time Warp and the regulars coming for the floor show. It showed clips of people announcing their number of showings. There were people dressed as Magenta and Colombia. We watched people cover up when the water guns fired. Ducking rice. Flipping toast into the air. I don't know if they showed newcomers being called virgins. This was the early eighties and we didn't say such things back then.

I was in love. It was interactive theater. It was everything a ten year old loved about kid's theater, except with more penis shaped exercise equipment. I didn't know I was seeing anything sexual or transgressive. I just liked the idea of throwing shit in the movies. Or talking back at the theater. Dancing on the seats. It seemed like the next logical step in the movie going experience. Watch the movie and then become the movie.

And hell, Tom Bosley gave his tacit approval, how bad could it really be?

3

A few years later, I watched the movie Fame on HBO, not sure if I liked the movie, but it was R rated, so I was for it. It showed kids not just going to Rocky Horror, but needing it. Growing from it. Being accepted because of it. I didn't want to be accepted in any small world, but there were scenes of women dressed in garter belts. I actually am not sure if I was aware that Dr. Frank N Furter was played by Tim Curry, a man. I might have thought he was just a butch woman. I was eleven and was pretty naive.

You must understand, that at this time, my favorite song was "Lola" by the Kinks. I would tell people how much I love that song. Because I had not dealt well with my father's death, I was going to a therapist. I told my therapist that it was the best song ever. She asked me what it was about. I told her it was about a shy guy who meets a very strong woman. I guess I always missed hearing the line in the song that stated, "I know what I am and I'm glad I'm a man, and so is Lola." The therapist must have written many things about me in her notes. The one thing that should have been written was, "Does not follow lyrics well."

I didn't know what Frank N Furter was. I didn't know myself well. I did know I wanted to see the movie. Whenever I went to downtown Nyack, our town, I would see the marquee for the Cinema East and underneath the letters that spelled out the movie for the week was "Roc Horror" in small, unmatched letters. It was there for years, until the movie started playing at the smaller Pearl River Theater, a few towns over.

My older sister talked about her friends going to Rocky. I wanted to go with her. My sister was, and still is, much cooler than me. I figured if I went with her, I might get some residual coolness.

The only negative thing about Rocky Horror I knew was that my mother wanted to go. If Rocky came up in conversation she always said that it seemed like fun and if me or my sister ever go, she would like to as well. Oh my god. Even at eleven, I knew that was an awful idea. For the length of time I went to Rocky Horror in my teens and early twenties, my mother would say on occasion that I should take her. Kill me. I think there was one time Tommy tried to get a family night going, where we regulars brought our folks. I told him my mother was busy that weekend, whatever weekend it might be.

4

If I was introduced to Rocky Horror by Tom Bosley, I became an expert about it from the library.

At 14, I got a part time job at the Valley Cottage Library. I was a page, which meant I put books back on the shelf. It was a small library and there were never enough returned books to shelve to fill up the entire two hour shift. Instead, I would have to organize shelves, making sure that the books were in the right location. That was horrible work.

Instead, I would hide in the 700s (art, entertainment and sports) or the 800s (poetry and plays) and read. If any supervisor came by, I would make like I was saving the books from being miss shelved.

One of the books I read was on Cult Movies. I have tried over the years to figure out which Cult Movie book it was and get a copy, but I have not been successful. I must have read the chapter on Rocky Horror a lot, because my memory of it is pretty strong. Maybe I only read it once and this was information my brain determined important to keep.

I read about how it all happened. I read how Richard O'Brien was fired from his role as Herod in Jesus Christ Superstar. How he thought it was a terrible rock musical because rock and roll must have sex in it. I agreed with his assessment. I learned how he wrote the Time Warp first. How he got the play The Rocky Horror Show up and running in a tiny theater in London. How it became the big thing for the chic people and those that wanted to be chic. How they got it in Los Angeles. How they put it on Broadway and why that was a flop. The making of the movie. The flop that was too. How several people started going to see it every night. I read about the first line shouted at the screen. "How strange was it?"

I learned about the African American movie executive, Ashely Boone, Jr, was the guy who made it a midnight movie. I learned that Boone was also the only 20th Century Fox executive to push for a movie called Star War. This guy was good and neither of these two movies would have been successful without him.

I learned about how it turned into a movie that some people needed to see again and again. How it changed itself into a community event. I learned a lot from that book. I wonder why this stayed with me. I can't remember details of what we did at Rocky or why it meant something to us, but this origin story is so clear. I remember where I stood in the library as I read it.

I love the idea that I was paid to read about Rocky Horror. I think it was minimum wage, which was $3.35 an hour. If I lingered for a half hour with that book, I was paid a buck sixty five for my time learning about Richard O'Brien and all that he made.

"I made you. And I can break you, just like that."

5

What I have laid out for you are pages of prologue. I have detailed all the ways that Rocky Horror played with my imagination all before I even saw the movie.

So it is with chagrin that I admit I don't have a strong memory of the first time I saw the Rocky Horror Picture Show. I have some clues. Some thoughts. I have memories of memories.

I feel like these stories always have that moment when the long dreamed of event occurs and the memoirist states, "I will never forget a moment of it. It has etched itself in my memory." And then the writer will go for pages with every minute detail. It was so important, how could the writer not have it all down?

Nothing of the sort was the case the first time I saw Rocky Horror.

I think it was after a high school play I was in. I might have been fifteen, which made it 1985. The movie was ten years old at that point. I was excited. I was finally going to see the movie.

I was told that I should not sit in the back row or the front row. Those are for regulars. I remember people shouting at the screen. I thought it was funny. Every time Janet's name was mentioned, people shouted, "Slut." For Brad, people said "Asshole." I got wet during the rain scene and there were people running around with water guns.

And I got up to do the Time Warp. It's what you do, I suppose.

And I was bored soon after. The movie made no sense. It looked cheap. The second half was a drag. It wasn't bad, I guess, it didn't have the good music that the first half had. And I was tired and it was after one o'clock and I wanted to go home.

When the movie ended on the dour, downbeat note, I was bummed. All this build up for a movie event and it was not a celebration. Everyone died. The last song was done by the narrator, who didn't even sing. He just recited the lines. "Crawling on the planet's face," indeed.

I did not leave jubilantly. I left because it was over and I told my mother I would be home by two and two o'clock was soon approaching.

If there were more details, they are gone.

Oh, I do remember one thing. There was a cartoon that ran before the movie. It was a Pink Panther cartoon. People shouted lines and comments about that cartoon as well. I do remember thinking it was cool that there was a cartoon, like movies had years ago. But leaving at the end, I realized that the cartoon made it a longer night.

And that was it. I had a teenage experience. One of those that I wasn't going to do again. I was able to say that I saw Rocky, and what was the big deal. I was too sophisticated for it.

I think a year later I went to see the movie again. Once more, it was after a high school play I was in. I think it was a thing theater folk thought we had to do. We put on a play, now let's see Rocky Horror. Everyone gets their ideas from the movie Fame, I suppose.

I don't remember a thing about the movie. My only memory of that night was going to the back-parking lot of the movie theater and drinking a can of Guinness with a kid named Nick. Maybe I figured if I got fucked up, the movie would be better. Didn't all the Rocky Horror people take drugs and drink to abandon? That must make the movie better.

This is how stupid we were. We thought the way to get drunk was to share one single can of stout. Yes. You should not drink Guinness from a can. I am aware of that now. We had some sips and it tasted like unfinished bread. It was lousy but I was game. Nick took his sip and spit it on the asphalt. "We can't drink this. This is shit." He then threw it in a dumpster. I was shocked. I didn't like it, but I was willing to drink it. We are at a crazed event, shouldn't we be fucked up? Even if we don't like the stuff that will fuck us up?

That is all I recall of the second time I saw Rocky Horror. The whole movie was nothing but an aftertaste of poor beer.

5

Facebook Messenger communication with Foster. April 20. 8:30 PM

David: I am drawing a blank. What was the cartoon that Cinema East played before Rocky Horror? Was it a Pink Panther cartoon?

Foster: In later years. In the beginning of our time it was something else. Something stupid with a yellow and tan palette. I'll see if I can figure it out.

David: What is it an Ant and Anteater cartoon where the anteater talks like Henny Youngman?

Foster: Yes!

6

So why did I start going to the movie on a regular basis? And why did I start to love it? Well, being able to get there and back was a big factor. So, after I started to drive, it became much more of a reality. I didn't have to worry about rides home. I certainly would never ask my mother for a ride.

But the main reason I fell into the scene was because of Tommy. Tommy was a friend and he had decided he loved Rocky Horror. It was the greatest thing in the world and he would call up and tell me I had to come. Tommy told me he started working at the Cinema East in Nyack and I should get a job there too. So, I quit my job at the library and started in the wonderful world of cinema. Was I that pliable? My friend told me to take a job and I did? Yeah, seems like I was a push over.

Tommy was excited about the world. He loved horror movies and loud rap music. He adored Kiss, the band. Don't ever diss Kiss in Tommy's vicinity. He was enthusiastic about so much. And working at the movie, he was enthusiastic about hanging with his friends and going to Rocky Horror after our shift. He had a large group of friends and they were all going to the movie. Or he made friends there. I was always in awe of his ability to talk to people, to be excited about new folk and to embrace them as long-lost companions. As I write this, I am amazed to realize that I am talking about a 16-year-old. Tommy was a shining star. He loved horse racing, boxing, extreme gore, loud metal, cheap beer and his friends (not in that order). Those who knew him, even a little bit, miss him all the more.

"Dave. You need to work at the movie theater." And so I did. This was the town movie. There used to be town movies. Cinema East was a beast. It had 700 seats for one screen. It's hard to imagine such opulence. But it wasn't opulent, it was never as clean as it should have been. How could it be? It was cleaned and maintained by teen idiots like us. Rob got Tommy a job. Tommy got me a job. Eventually we got Foster, Paul and David S gigs.

Foster was the star. Or rather, Foster could play responsible better than the rest of us. He soon became Assistant Manager of the theater. He also made sure that the stealing was done appropriately and would not allow us to be caught. Yes, there was stealing. There was rampant reselling of tickets. The way it was worked is that someone bought a ticket for the movie. They brought it into the theater and it was ripped. But in the scheme, the ticket was not ripped and it was then brought to the guy working the box office and it was resold. That ticket was not part of the tally, so it was extra money. Free money. Our money.

I never did it. I was too uncomfortable with that. (The story of my life) But I reaped the benefits. They bought me Chinese food during dinner break. And because I was the only one with a senior license that allowed driving after 9 PM, I was the designated Rocky driver. The boys would throw me twenties for gas money. No one was innocent.

Rocky was always the destination. Foster or Tommy would announce that we were going to Rocky and everyone would change from the popcorn stained work clothes and jump into my beat-up Mustang and I would drive us to Pearl River. That's where Rocky played. I think we even got in for free because it was the same theater chain.

And that's how Rocky Horror became part of my life. I was the getaway driver.

7

Pearl River, New York. 1986.

I have heard about a lot of different weekly showings of Rocky back when it was alive and thriving. I have been to a few myself and they were all well run. There was a hierarchy. People ran the show. They were in the front row. They made sure that people didn't over shout the lines. They arranged for the props to be there and for things to happen in logical ways. "You have the toast? Good. Make sure you give them out to people." "What do you mean the water gun is filled with vodka? Well drink it now and fill it with water." "You are running the time warp today." They would make the announcements before the movie started. They did the anniversaries and the humiliation of the newcomers, shouting "Virgin" at them. They had a good relationship with the theater managers. They created a show. The really good ones made it a safe, open space (as much as anyone talked about safety and spaces all the way back in the grungy 80s).

The Rocky Horror at Pearl River was more disheveled. There were regulars, but there was mostly a sense of seeing who showed up and let's put on a show. Not much was planned. Not much went correctly. Tommy would shout out and be loud and welcoming. He was everybody's ambassador. No one seemed to be steering the ship though.

Somewhere in that year, a guy brought a shit load of toilet paper to be thrown. Someone looked at it and said, "Wouldn't it be funny if we wrapped up someone in toilet paper and that would be Rocky as the mummy." (For those who don't remember, the monster Rocky was wrapped up before he was animated) And for some dumb reason, I said, "I'll do it." Maybe Tommy talked me into it. If he did it, it probably wasn't hard to convince me.

So, I stripped down to my shorts and several drunken teens twisted toilet paper around me. I couldn't move because if I even twitched, the one ply toilet paper would rip and they would have to start all over again.

They then put me on their shoulders and carried me up to the front of the theater at the right time of the movie. (I was a skinny thing. I was six foot and about 130 pounds. I was a kid always in desperate need of a sandwich.) I remember thinking, "Shit. Those assholes are going to drop me." It was a long walk up to the front. One guy, the one with little teeth, said, "I'm getting tired, I think Dave's gonna slip."

That was Rocky Horror for me, a bad idea followed by fear and panic.

I got to the front. They righted me to my feet. Then they unwrapped me in a poor approximation of what was happening on the screen. Then I was free and wearing only khaki shorts. I ran around the theater singing "The Sword of Damocles" as much as I could, because I really didn't know the words. None of us liked that song. Why would I know one of the shitty ones? I performed the three minute song with as much gusto as I had. I was playing a muscle man, me, a walking example of Charles Atlas's before picture.

I can only imagine what the people in the theater thought. For most people coming, this was a sometime thing. They might think it fun to check out that midnight movie people are always going on about. They had no skin in the game. They went a time or two and then they were done. "I saw it, it was okay." They probably were expecting people dressed up as Columbia, Magenta or Riff Raff. They were probably expecting the Pride Parade Goes to the Movies. It must have been disappointing to discover a bevy of obnoxious kids dressed in whatever we dressed in all the time. We were not special. Just a bunch of kids. (I will say this again, but this is all about the one we went to. I heard about other theaters that put on Rocky and it was full of costumes and outrageousness. We were the burbs. We were soaking in it.)

The regulars were in charge of shouting out the lines louder than anyone else. And for that, I was good at it. I had a loud voice. I still do, but now I use that power only for good.

8

Here was a day in the life of a teenaged Rocky goer. This was not a typical day. But it was one that remains with me.

Saturday night. Tommy and I went to work and then immediately were sent to the 303 Drive-In. The small chain owned all of the three drive-ins. Working the drive-ins sucked. No one hired for them stayed. I think the average lifespan of a drive-in worker was three weeks. They were trained, then they worked for a week, and then they trained their replacement. I say trained while biting my lip.

There was no training involved. After one day, they put me on the griddle making burgers. I must have made the worst burgers ever eaten. Though no one complained. Why would anyone complain about food at a drive-in? The place was located right next to an active county landfill. It always reeked. No one could notice that I cooked the burgers poorly.

Several employees quit every weekend, which meant we who worked at other theaters in the chain were sent to fill in the gaps. I had a car. I was always screwed. At least this time I had Tommy with me. He was friends with everyone still remaining at the drive-in. He was friends with everyone.

He wanted me to go to Rocky that night and then go to a toga party at some guy's apartment in South Nyack that was starting at 3 AM after Rocky. I surprised myself by saying no. I was going on a trip with the boy scouts in three days (yes, I was a boy scout. That will be another book.) and I wanted to get some sleep. "Come on Dave," Tommy said in the passenger that rocked back and forth due to a blown bolt. "It will be so much fun."

It was a warm night and the drive-in was packed. We worked the box office. We went to each car, counted out how many people were there and charge 4.50 a head. We were offered beer and pot if we would let them slip in without paying. One drunk girl offered me a cuddle and a kiss if she could get in free. I was too dumb and innocent to realize the advantages to my position. Sometimes, feeling scared and godlike, I would wave cars in just because I could.

An hour in, the torrential rain came and hit us and we were soaked. Tommy came to me. "Dave, I need the keys for your car."

"Why the fuck do you need my car? You are not leaving me here."

"No, that lady over there with her daughter needs a jump. Here battery died. And I think they can hear you so watch your language." Saying this made Tommy laugh.

"Be careful with it." I gave him my keys. And I watched him drive my car right into a fence. I went over and swore at him like a mad man. I pulled him out of the car.

"Dave, you're swearing in front of that family," was all Tommy said to me. Boy did I ever swear. I drove my car and helped the woman recharge her battery. I am sure I became one of the stories of why going to a drive-in with her daughter was such a bad choice.

I was on edge. I could feel the Hyde in me coming out. I had sworn in front of children. I had turned down a kiss from a drunk girl. I was not seeing a good end to the night.

One of the owners came to the box office a little bit later and told Tommy, "We're quieting down. Why don't you leave, we're all set." He pointed to me. "You can have him go too, Tommy."

Tommy put his arm around me and steered me to my car. "Dude. We are done. You need to relax. You need to go to Rocky. It will settle your nerves."

"Rocky will settle my nerves?"

"Works every time."

"Fine, but I am not going to the toga party. I have to get some sleep tonight."

"You bet."

It was a wonderful time at Rocky, meaning that it was a time I was in the front row and I felt like Transylvanian royalty. Everyone wanted to be in the front row. The guy without the teeth was running the show that night, it seemed. Some women (I call them women because they were like in their twenties) came up to the guy and he hugged them and told them they should sit in the front row. All the seats were taken. He took one of them and pushed her in the seat I was in. We shared it together.

I didn't know what to do. There was a woman crushed up against me. Should I put my arm around her? Should I rest my hand on her thigh? Should she I and do the Time Warp together? I was turned on and petrified. We did do the Time Warp together. It might have been the first time I did the Time Warp with a partner. It might be sad to admit, but it was easier doing the Time Warp as a solo.

I didn't do anything else with her. I never learned her name. I couldn't be forward with an older woman who was a stranger to me. Okay. That made no sense. But it was where my tangled thoughts led me.

After the movie was over, Tommy asked me, "So you want to go to the toga party."

"No. I have to work twelve hours tomorrow and then I got to get ready for my trip. I have to get some sleep, Tommy."

"I hear that girl you were sitting with is going to the party."

"Alright. I can go."

She didn't go to the party. Of course. There were ten or so people dressed in bed sheets. I refused. I was so terrified about everything that I seemed like I had principles. Dirty movies played on the TV. One guy got so drunk that he passed out and people took pictures of him with Cheetos up his nose.

There were naked people running around. I was drinking beer like it was a homework assignment. I didn't want to do it, but I was expected to. I drank like I was cramming for a pop quiz.

Sometime in that late hour, with a girl I knew from school leaning up against me. I took a deep breath and kissed her, expecting that I was going to have to apologize for it. And she kissed me back. She tasted of nicotine and possibility.

Don't dream it. Be it.

Things got sloppy at the party after that. But that's not what I want to talk about right now. What I want to talk about was when dawn broke and Foster and Tommy came to me and said we should go to Cinema East. We were all three assigned to start at ten in the morning. We might as well go there and get some sleep on the lobby couches. Foster was the assistant manager and had keys.

We stopped at Dunkin Donuts for sugar and caffeine. We laid out on the couches and tried to sleep. We laughed and sang Rocky songs. Then Foster and Tommy found a way to pass out. They both snored.

I was awake. I was swirling with the last twelve hours and all the things I didn't understand. I spent the next hour trying to clean the auditorium by myself. But all the spilled soda, flung popcorn and scattered wrappers beat me at every corner. It was as much a mess as when I started. I woke the boys at ten and we finished the clean-up in another hour. During the clean-up, Tommy played the Rocky Horror soundtrack. He and I sang along like our lives depended on it.

"Flow morphia slow, let the sun and light come streaming into my life."

Just another night at Rocky.

9

My time at Rocky slowed at the end of the summer, not because school was coming back, but because we all got fired from the movie theater. We didn't get fired. We got transferred to the drive-in. No one ever survived the drive-in, so we quit before we even started there. Which is what management wanted. They found out about the ticket scam and called us all bad apples. Foster stayed on. And I was hired back too, because no one could imagine that I was one of the thieves. That hurt my feelings a bit. I could be a thief; I could be a villain.

But Tommy and the others were gone. No one trusted us. And with that, the real thrust of Rocky Horror disappeared. I still went. But it was easier to beg off staying out so late when it was Tommy calling me on the phone. It was harder to say no when we were selling popcorn and cleaning up sick on the bathrooms.

I tried to get some of my geeky friends, the ones that hung out in the computer lab to go with me a few times, but there was no chance of that. In my senior year, I probably added 7 or 8 more showings to my number. My amorphous, uncertain number. But I didn't feel part of it because I was not part of all the stories from the last weekend or the weekend before that. I was not attending regularly. I was not privy to the secret handshake.

Tommy and Foster kept going. The movie was important to them. I would go sometimes because they were important to me.

10

On going to college in Massachusetts, I became a Rocky Horror snob. I was not into seeing the movie. I was into the different soundtrack versions. And it was all on CD. I was so cutting edge with my new technology. I had a milk cart filled with what I thought was great music. I had REM and Thelonious Monk. Everyone will love me when they see the music I'm digging.

But the gems of the collection were all my Rocky Horror soundtracks. There was the motion picture soundtrack, which was okay. It was decent, but it didn't have all the songs, like Planet Schmanet Janet. And Barry Bostwick and Susan Sarandon were not as good in the songs as the others. The others were from the theater productions. Bostwick and Sarandon were Hollywood hired guns. They just didn't have the chops. So said 19 year old me. Can a dork be a snob?

I had a few other soundtracks. My favorite was the Roxy. That was the first American production and had Tim Curry and Meatloaf in it. The music was tight. The guy playing Riff Raff did quite a different take on the Time Warp. I liked the songs cut out of the movie like Once in a While and the full version of Superheroes. That one was played the most by me in the dorms.

The only thing I didn't like about the album was the cover. It had a garish illustration of Columbia. It was like a German Expressionist take on Rocky Horror. Someone even gave me a copy of that illustration as a poster for a present. They figured that I love Rocky, so I will love all images of Rocky. I still own that poster, which I don't think I ever hung up. I won't throw it out. It is still a memento from my Rocky years. But now it holds pride of place in a pile of other posters up in the attic.

I also had, but rarely played, the original London Production for 1973. This was the earliest production. I know it had Curry and O'Brien in it. It just didn't sound good to me. It was messy and off key and I was such a snob. I would play it sometimes to prove that I was a big Rocky fan. I had it ready to show off to people, to let them know that I had rare recordings. Shockingly, no one ever showed interest in it.

One recording I never got was the audience participation album. It was the film, with all the call and response included. I heard it a bunch of times when I worked at Cinema East. Tommy had a tape and played it while we cleaned the auditorium. It was weird. It was several years old at this point and it felt dated. The jokes were so 1981. It was not as hip as us kids from five years in the future. And really, what was the point? To learn the lines so you will be ready the next time you go to Rocky?

But the thing was, you weren't ready. If you copied the audience participation album, you were doing lines that weren't from your Rocky. We talked about local lines. We had them. We created our own thing. The Pearl River theater was small and it was hidden away in Rockland County New York, but we were unique.

That record was a souvenir record. Something to remind you of the good time you had once. It was not anything I wanted to relive. I wanted to be there with my vision of Rocky Horror or I could just stay in my dorm and play the soundtrack. The Roxy version though. That one was the best. Or at least, that's what I know to be true.

11

There was a small science fiction convention at my college. I was very lonely that first year. Of course I went.

I met her on the first day of the convention at a screening of Santos vs the Vampire Queen. We talked throughout the movie. We were shushed constantly. We spent the rest of the convention together.

She was older. 24. She had a real job working for some foundation on the MIT campus. I felt honored she wanted to talk to me. She spoke of her time at Rocky Horror in Cambridge. It was one of the best known Rocky shows. I was humbled. She namedropped the big names in the Rocky scene. I didn't know them.

On the last night of the convention, we crushed into a hotel room where Rocky Horror was playing. We shouted lines. I realized my lines didn't jibe with what everyone else was saying. I kept quiet and listened.

She told me it was getting uncomfortable in the room. I wanted to stay. The song, Sweet Transvestite, was fast approaching. She said she was leaving then. I left with her.

In the hallway she stopped and looked at me in my eyes. She looked. I had no idea what the look was. Was it a kiss she wanted? Only one way to find out.

I leaned down and kissed her. From the hotel room was the deep voice of an old friend. "I'm not much of a man, by the light of day, but by night I'm one hell of a lover."

12

Somewhere in my first year of college, Rocky Horror moved from the Pearl River Theater back to the Cinema East in Nyack. That was a big deal. It was a bigger theater. And it was our hometown. No more driving a half hour to Pearl River. Now we could stumble home. Or get so drunk and not worry about being stranded in a different town. Now at least we could be stranded in our own town.

My memory makes me realize that I went a lot more with it at the Cinema East. I was there every time I was home from college. I was there during summer break. There was no way I could be considered important to the show. I was just the kid home from school. Both Foster and Tommy lived in Nyack. For some time there, they actually had an apartment together downtown.

Rocky was fun in Nyack. The space was huge. There was a lot of running around. There seemed to be a lot of people.

I remember one time, Foster and I went to the movies at Cinema East, just to see the flick. It was When Harry Met Sally. We brought a bottle of vodka. Somewhere near the end of the movie I passed out. I woke up to see Rocky Horror happening. The guys who were working the theater knew I was going to stay for Rocky and didn't kick me out.

One day, Foster let me know that things were going to change. "I got a call from someone who runs the floor show at a different theater. That place decided to stop playing Rocky."

"Was it not doing well."

"No, it had a big following. I think the theater didn't want the hassle. Who wants to clean up puke and rice and toast every weekend? Anyway, they are a floorshow in search of a Rocky. They asked if they could join ours. I said sure. It's not like I could stop them if I wanted to."

And that's how the Cinema East's Rocky got a big burst of people. These people were dedicated. They had costumes. They had people who sung along. There were good looking people dressed in garters showing up at midnight ready to put on a show.

I have said before that I loved the friends and the shouting at the screen. This was the first time I saw a produced floor show. A real one with a set cast. I was nonplussed. It seemed odd to me. I didn't know what I was supposed to focus on. Was I to look at the people in front of the front row in costumes dancing about? The lighting was not great and they were hard to see. Or should I look at the movie? What was the purpose of the floor show? Everyone seemed to be having a good time and the audience cheered them on, so what did it matter if I liked it or not?

The new people were good after I got to know them. A few of them even came to my house. They liked my dedication to shouting the lines. I was amazed when I would hang with them after the movie and they were out of their costumes. They were like different people. More. They were like aliens. I was not sure which was their real clothes. Their real skin.

One time I played in the floor show with these talented, dedicated people. One of them cursed and said that the Brad wasn't going to make it. "I'll do it," I said.

And like that. I was Brad. It was a lot of tedious work to be Brad dancing and singing and looking uncomfortable. I didn't even have to act. At the big finale, I was down to my underwear. I was uncomfortable at first. But then it was fine. I wasn't naked after all. I was a poor Brad, but at least the show was able to go on.

I got in the habit of sitting by myself in the middle of the auditorium and shouting out lines to my heart's content. I was a loud voice everyone could hear. I was taking a solo. I was improvisational jazz. I was kidding myself.

Sometime in the early nineties, Cinema East closed. It was getting impossible for independent theater owners to survive. I think Rocky

Horror ended before that. It's hard for me to be sure. I had stopped going to Rocky already.

13

And this is where the narrative thrust of our accounting ends. There is no way to make this a story, a linear telling. What remains are a series of snapshots. I have scattered memories from now on. If you were looking for some a to b to c story, then you probably have never seen Rocky.

The part that is surprising to me is what is missing from this telling. It is all choice. It is all what I decide I would like to tell.

There is not a lot of discussion here about the movie itself. I feel like I am leaving those who don't know the film in the dark. That's fine if you need to think that this is about Rocky Horror Picture Show at all.

The history of midnight movies and this movie in particular is worth recounting. There are books and blogs that can be found about all those things.

There is also little discussion of sex. How can there be a discussion of Rocky Horror shows and no salacious back row shenanigans? I am as surprised as you. As I write this, I find that I rather not go into detail. I am not denying that there was sex and flirtation. I am just saying that I would rather you just assume it. Let's work together on this one. I could tell you of relationships that began and flamed to conclusion as the movie played. I could tell you of hickeys and people jumping into someone's lap. There were explorations and experimentations that happened in a place that allowed such things to occur. All of these are not in these pages. But I trust you. I know that you are smart and can fill in those blanks.

14

I asked Foster why he kept going to Rocky Horror. He replied. "I kept doing it because I felt like I belonged there, more than anywhere else. I was shy. Much worse than I let on. The movie was the distraction that allowed me to be myself. Maybe because no matter what I did to call attention to myself, nobody was looking at me. Not really. I could be on the stage, facing a crowd, beer in hand, screaming vulgarities and still not have to be the center of attention. My favorite weekly moment was the diving scores because it consistently got a laugh from visitors. My favorite single moment was probably the realization of the fact that we were a community. We had the toga party and people from Rocky came. It was bigger than two hours twice a week. My time at Rocky at Cinema East (and Pearl River to a lesser extent) remains one of my favorite things I've done in my life."

15

It really needs to be stated that this was before streaming. That goes without saying. But this was even before the time that Rocky was on video. I don't know what the hold-up was, but the only way to see the movie was to go to a theater at midnight. We were all bummed we couldn't watch the movie every day, but it added the mystique of it. It made it precious.

Around 1990, I got a copy. It was a bootleg VHS tape from a Japanese laser disc. I think I spent the insane price of twenty-five dollars for it. There were Japanese subtitles. It added to the ambience.

Here is the funny thing about purchasing movies. You think that you will watch them all the time. The outlay is justified because I will be seeing it like two or three times a week. That's not true. I figure I watched that video of Rocky about ten times, on the outside. I could still see it in the theaters back then.

And besides, watching it home is wrong. You can shout at the screen, but that doesn't make you part of a community, it makes you kind of insane.

The last time I think I played that video was late 92 or early 93. I was with Tommy at his tiny apartment. He had a new girlfriend (later his wife) and the two of them invited me to come over with the tape. She had never seen Rocky and he wanted to lay it on her. There was another woman there. I don't know if that was a set-up for me, but nothing came of it. Instead we became close friends for a time.

We first watched Frankenhooker, a great and disgusting comedy. It was the only other movie I saw at a midnight screening. Then we played Rocky. In this tiny space, Tommy and I shouted lines and acted out the participation parts. We even dragged the women up on their feet to do the Tme Warp.

I am pretty sure, Tommy did the jump on me, to mimic Frank-n-Furter jumping on Rocky at the end of the Charles Atlas song.

This was all to accompany a poor-quality image on a 19 inch television screen, with Japanese subtitles.

Years later, the woman who was there told me that they thought Tommy and I were fucking crazy. They could not get over the fact that we were jumping on each other and shouting so loud. It was a small room, why would anyone think they needed to be so boisterous?

I had no good answer to that. I mean, I did have an honest answer to that, but it was never a good one.

16

There is a major aspect of seeing Rocky at Cinema East I did not mention, getting food afterwards at Hogan's.

Janet Hogan's Diner was an institution. It was a 24 hour old school (3000 page menu) place that had a bar and enough parking for everyone wanting sustenance at 2:30 in the morning.

Its sign said. "Where the Elite Meet to Eat." It was a line we said often. We are the elite. We eat at Hogan's.

The food was good enough. Are you wanting fine cuisine after dancing the Time Warp all night?

The waitresses were a few steps away from surly. They never pushed us out. There could be five to twenty people from Rocky showing up. Some straggled in. Some never made the three-mile trek. Forever lost.

This was the evening's epilogue. We talked about how the show went. We waxed nostalgic about other Rocky's we had seen. How we could do it better. How we should keep it the same. This was where the last chance hook-ups happened. If you didn't make it at the theater, you might have that chance over a greasy burger. The burgers were so amazingly greasy.

I remember one evening when Tommy and others were talking about homemade tattoos. Everyone was pulling up sleeves to show their handiwork.

For most of us, this was our chance to come down from whatever elevated place we were at for the ride home. For the bed we planned to collapse in.

Hogan's was purchased to make way for a giant mall. The mall project stalled, so for years, the empty husk of Hogan's stayed there, mocking us. It still told us that it was where the elite met to eat. But we knew that was just a lie. Another tease in a life of bump and grind.

17

He came up to me in the middle of the screening. I was losing interest in the film. Around the time of Sword of Damocles, people started conversations, some just split. The second half of the movie is not as strong as the first. And if you are seeing it scores of times, you are well aware of that. Hell, my favorite song in the second half isn't even on the soundtrack album, "Planet Shmanet Janet." So, it is not surprising I was looking ready to be bothered.

I knew him from high school. He was kind of a friend. He asked me if I wanted to get high. Fuck yeah. He said he only had roaches and that he would have to shot gun the joint hit. I was not savvy, and he had to explain it to me.

He would have to inhale the hit and then blow it toward my mouth while I inhaled. Ooooo-kay. We went into the fire exit hallway and lit up and he blew smoke into my mouth.

He kept on leaning in closer and closer. His mouth was a whisper from mine. I was dumb. I was not aware of this. He was going in for a kiss. I leaned back, stumbling my feet for some space. I was embarrassed. He seemed fine. "Do you want some more? I can blow another hit if you want."

I was happy to be high. I thanked him. I went back to my seat. I wondered if I was obligated to kiss him for the free smoke. I wasn't sure. I was annoyed that the only way he thought I would kiss him is by getting me stoned. Was I flattered? Was I annoyed? Was I wasted from the second hand high? If there were rules of etiquette that covered such a situation, no one had shown me them.

18

From Facebook Messenger with Foster on March 20th, 2020

David: There was a line that we used to say during the song "Sweet Transvestite." When Tim Curry sang, "So, you've been caught with a flat" we would shout out, "How'd you know that?" I loved that line. It always made me laugh. Was that a line that you came up with? Did you make it up?

Foster: Don't remember hearing it elsewhere, so I think it was a local line. But I really couldn't say for sure..

David: I love the local lines. I love how things shifted from place to place. From location to location.

Foster: I didn't like one of our local lines. (when Riff Raff turns the ray gun on Dr. Scott at the end of the movie) "Kill the cripple. They get all the best parking spots."

19

The lines were my favorite part. I liked saying them with other like it was a church call and response. I liked that chant. That holy doctrine.

But saying a line on my own was just a joy. If I got a laugh. All the better. Foster said he loved doing the diving scores because it always got a laugh. I loved lines that could surprise people. Make them break out with laughter. It was a great job to have.

I have always wondered if some folklorist ever got a chance to record the different Rocky's and analyze the lines said. What was always the same, ("This man has no fucking neck!") and which were just for that one place in time. ("Ladies and gentleman, the Nyack Police Department!")

Some of the lines that I still feel compelled to shout out are steeped in the seventies and eighties. "We are the world!" "It's Betty Ford before the surgery. It's Betty Ford after surgery." "Na-nu, na-nu."

We used to shout out a line that was an inside joke. The line was supposed to be about the close up of Susan Sarandon's feet encased in panty hose. "Her toes look like cheese doodles!" One night, Foster was drunk and said, "Her cheese looks like toes doodles." We liked that so much, we kept that as the line instead. The visitors to the movie probably thought we were all stupid.

We were all stupid.

Then came the questionable lines, like the one Foster still regrets. "Kill the cripples." Even then, we knew it was an awful line. But we said it, because we were young and thought ourselves transgressive. And because that was the line and we said the lines. We didn't question them.

And though some might disagree, I think some of the lines painted us in a poor light. Replaying them in my head, I am struck with a reactionary bent to many of them.

Rocky Horror is a wonderfully queer movie. You don't get more queer than this flick. It was 1975 and there was no denying the pansexuality of the film. Sure, there is a slight bit of "bury your gays" in the film with the killing of Frank at the end. But for the most part, the fierce performance of Tim Curry is what you remember.

So how is it that some of our lines were quite fearful of homosexuality?

When Frank pushes Brad into a compromising position and asks, "Would Janet like to see you like this?" Our response was, "No, and we don't either."

"Brad, you're a fag for his tool."

There were others that I am not recalling, which is fine by me. Look, I don't know how it happened, but we were mostly a hetero normative group. For a movie that attracted and nourished so much of the LGBTQ community, I don't understand how we had such aggression in what we were saying.

It was the middle of the eighties. There was a hell of a lot of fear with AIDS and the reactionary Reagan administration. We were also in a pretty Republican county a bit north of New York City. Maybe it stood to reason that we showed some of our dumb youthful stupidity.

To be fair, there were some vulgar lines said towards women and hetero sex. In Janet's song "Touch Me," we would shout out, "Drill me, fill me and bill me."

I could be wrong. But when I hear other people shout out lines they grew up saying, I am struck by the vulgar aggression in the ones that I learned. I try to not shout them out, but it's like instinct. Like the patella tendon being struck. I struggle against so much reflex. So much learned behavior.

20

After its demise as a movie house, the Cinema East was transformed into a community theater. I never saw a play or show there, which I think was one of the reasons it didn't succeed. No one saw plays or shows there.

There was one final time I was in the lobby of that old movie theater. I was told of a play reading series that the theater was doing in the lobby. They never got enough people in attendance to use the auditorium, so they put chairs in the lobby. It was big enough for that.

The play reading series was run by actors who appeared in the soap opera, The Guiding Light. The actors met to work on their theater chops in between episodes. Many of the actors lived near Nyack, so they would do staged readings of old plays there. This time was "Crimes of the Heart."

There were about 25 people in attendance. All the soap opera actors entered together in a pack, as if they felt safer in numbers. As soon as they came in, several of those in attendance squealed, boisterous delight. They stood up and approached the actors with pen and autograph books in hand. Several of the actors flinched backwards.

They performed the play seated in a row of chairs before us. They were great. They seemed excited to form the words written for them at this moment.

As enjoyable as this was, I found my mind wandering. I started looking around me. Over on those benches were where Foster and Tommy fell asleep after the toga party. Over there, near the bathrooms once stood a second concession stand we called The Bahamas. None of us liked being stuck there. And past the actors, through those shut doors, was the auditorium. We watched Rocky there. We made lives there. Past those doors, we created new roles of ourselves. We all danced to our own bejeweled floor show.

The theater did not survive. Now it is empty, a victim of flood and disregard.

22

The last time I spoke back at the movie was Halloween, 2015. I have hosted poetry shows at a bar in Worcester, Massachusetts for years and they asked me to host their Halloween party and costume contest. I was told to be there at nine with my part starting at ten. When I came in, the performance area was filled with costumed drinkers silently watching Rocky Horror on a projection screen. The bartender said, "It's kind of quiet. You go on after the movie."

I was mystified, "Sean, why the fuck is no one doing anything? They're watching Rocky like it's just a movie. What the fuck?"

"Maybe they don't know any better."

"Well, fuck that." I got a beer and proceeded to do all the lines. It was amazing. I remembered them all. I missed a few, but back when I was a kid, I also missed a few. People were laughing at what I was doing. Some were shocked. It was not a real Rocky Horror, but it was closer than just watching the damned thing in silence.

After that, I did the costume contest and did some games and then several people asked to watch Rocky Horror because they came in late. So,starting at 11, I did the whole show again. My voice was shot for days. But I was happy. It was only a month since Tommy died. I wasn't able to go to his funeral. I figured this was celebration enough. He would have been pleased.

At closing time, Sean the bartender said, "You did great. Man, you knew the whole movie. You must have seen it a lot."

"I've seen it a couple times."

21

When mentioning Rocky Horror to others, I sometimes get the reply, "Don't dream it. Be it." Yes. It is a very positive statement. Of course, Richard O'Brien got the line from a Frederick's of Hollywood catalog.

Even the best of advice can turn out to be ad copy.

Everything is marketed.

Even Rocky Horror. It is a big deal. It has been on Broadway. There is a Rocky Horror lunch box. There are toys and comic books. It isn't a licensing sensation like the Simpsons or Peanuts, but you can find your official Rocky Horror products if you just spend a tiny bit of time rummaging.

It's a badge of identification. It is a talisman. How we are to be. What we believe in. What speaks to us. What truth can we boil down into a wearable icon?

Every October, many theater companies put on The Rocky Horror Show for the big Halloween production.

In 2016, they made a TV movie remake. The cool thing was casting a trans actor as Frank N Furter, Laverne Cox. Cox was fantastic.

I was excited when it came on. My wife was away. My son was asleep. I was allowed to be as Rocky Horror geeky as I could.

And, it was missing something. The timing was off. The sexiness was muted. The way they tried to bring audience participation was misguided. While it was on, I went to my computer and started watching clips of the original movie on YouTube. I was singing along. I was shouting lines. And I was thinking of Tommy.

22

From Facebook Messenger on April 22, 2020.

David: I swear, this will be the last question. What do you think Tommy would have thought of the Rocky remake? We both know he would have watched it.

Foster: Man that's a tough one. The movie is so personal for so many people and I don't really know why it was for him. I appreciate the new film because I love musicals. I have listened to a lot of versions of the show because I love the songs and appreciate hearing slightly different takes on them. but I also listen to a LOT of covers of other songs I like. Sometimes I spent a whole day exploring a couple of songs on YouTube. I don't know if Tommy would like that. I like to see as many different bands as I can and eat in different restaurants. Drink different beers. Tommy followed KISS like Christ. He found something he loved and stuck with it. So my gut says that he probably would have found something positive to say but overall wouldn't have liked that they did it.

23

I got a text one Saturday morning from Foster. It was September 2015. "Tommy is not going to last much longer. We are driving up to see him this afternoon. You should come down and go with us."

I drove down from Massachusetts. Then Foster, David S and I drove up to Tommy's. He had been sick for a long time with cancer. He lasted much longer than anyone believed possible. This was where the impossible story ended.

In the car, we talked of light things. David S had been on a cooking competition show up in Canada. We talked about our families. A little bit about our jobs. And then we arrived at Tommy's.

He was lying on a hospital bed in the middle of the room, with a boxing match playing on the large TV. He talked of his love of boxing. He talked about the last time he saw the band Kiss. His daughter helped him drink root beer from a straw. We stayed for about an hour. He might not have known we were there. One of us kissed him on the cheek. Someone said we can't kiss him, because his system is so fragile.

We didn't say much on the way back to Nyack. I got in my car and drove back to Massachusetts. Somewhere in Connecticut, it dawned on me that we didn't talk about Rocky Horror with him. There was so much we didn't bring up with him.

Tommy died September 27th, 2015. He was 45 years old.

24

For a brief time, my friends and I found solace and joy in Rocky Horror. This little remembrance, this is my Rocky Horror. This is not the Rocky Horror story. I am sure it is not your Rocky Horror story, either. Just one of them.

I hope all those who needed the sense of community and freedom found it there. I still love the songs. I still love the anticipation I felt as I waited for the film to start. I still love so much about the movie.

I don't know how many times I have seen it. Those are just numbers. That's the wrong kind of math to calculate the worth of a film, of a show, of a piece of a life.

The last line of the movie is "Lost in time and lost in space and meaning."

That's not true, though. There is meaning. And we are not lost. We hear someone singing a familiar song and we will follow that voice. They will get us out of the darkness by singing.

"There's a light, over at the Frankenstein Place."

Completed April 22, 2020, 9:30 PM

Walking and Reading

Started Thursday June 25, 2020, 7:35 PM

1

The dog was fine.

Whenever I tell this story, the only thing people want to know about is the dog. So I will say it right in the first sentence. I will repeat it again. The dog was fine. He stood above my crumpled form and wondered what the hell was going wrong with the walk. One minute, we were walking, like we do. The next moment, I am down on the ground and he is patiently waiting for us to continue. Soon we will be getting home and that means a bowl of dog food. Walks are great. Why were we not walking then?

See. The dog was fine.

When anyone saw me in the next few weeks and wondered why I looked crooked, and walked with unpleasant deliberateness, I would say, "I got hit by a car while walking the dog."

I was never allowed to finish the sentence before the person would shout out, "Oh my god, how's the dog? Is he okay?"

The dog is fine.

"Oh thank god. Oh yeah, I hope you are okay too."

"I'll live."

Actually, the moment after I was hit by the car and was in the air, arcing up and then down, I wondered if I would live. So this is how it feels. I am going to land soon. Am I going to hit my head and die? Are these all the thoughts I will be allowed? Is this going to be the last thing I think of? I was sort of disappointed with myself.

I didn't have any great thoughts. A sense of the universe did not open up to me.

I did not think of my loved ones.

I did not think of the dog.

I only thought, I dropped my book. I'm going to lose my place in the story.

2

People asked me a good deal of questions. When they found out I was hit while walking the dog and reading a book at the same time. They asked me if I blacked out. They asked me if I was getting better. They asked me if I was going to get some money from insurance. They asked me what kind of idiot read a book while walking the dog.

The one question that was not asked of me was, "What was the book you were reading?"

No one seemed to find that important. I couldn't understand that with all the questions, no one seemed concerned with the story I was reading. What was wrong with people? Couldn't they realize what the important parts of a car accident were?

3

My Life as a Walking Reader: A List of Firsts

First time I remember reading and walking: 2002. I might have done it before that, but I don't remember it. I am sure there were times when I read an article I couldn't wait to read. Or a comic book I just purchased from the convenience store spinner rack on the one mile walk home. But it was in my early thirties that walking and reading became a thing.

First time someone gave me shit for walking and reading: 2002, the same month I really started doing it. I was 31 and I was on an hour break from my job and decided that I really wanted to continue reading the anthology of solo theater scripts I was into. I walked by two town employees working on filling in potholes. I nodded at them and then I heard them talking to each like from a collection of Pinter plays (which I read the week before). "Is he reading?" "He's reading." "Why is he reading?" "I don't know." "It must be a good book." "Must be," "I never needed to read a book that much." "I don't read much." "He is going to run into something." "He is definitely going to get hurt." "Yeah." "I ain't never seen anything like it." I don't know if this was a real conversation they would have with each other or if it was just for my benefit. I have always loved the way they gave me shit. I strive to be as wonderfully obtuse as these two were. Maybe me liking what they had to say is a good indication that I never learned my lesson.

The first time I was required to walk a dog on a regular basis: 2014. I love him to pieces now. But when we first got Fitzgibbons I was not prepared for the odd behavior of a rescue dog. He would bark, growl and bare his teeth at me. I was not very into him. It was my wife and son who wanted the dog. When he started being aggressive at me, I wasn't sure if we should have him. But my family informed me that if there was a choice between me and the dog, I would not be wise to put my money down on me. That day, I found a dog trainer and soon enough things got better. Yes, it's hard for me to see my life without Fitz, but back then I was happy to live in a dogless house.

The first time I read while walking with the dog: about a month after we got the pooch. It was part of the dog training. No, the reading was not part of the training. But I was told to increase my time walking him. The trainer sketched out a walk where I would go back and forth without any rhyme or reason. I would walk five steps and turn and then walk eleven steps and turn. Sometimes I had to walk clockwise, sometimes it was counter clockwise. My job was to be unpredictable. This fostered a need to trust me for the dog. It worked. But it was also kind of boring. I had to do this for fifteen minutes several times a day. I would put the leash on him and see a nearby book. Why not? I remember one of the first books I read while walking with Fitz was Joyland by Stephen King. I was listening to it as an audiobook in the car and I was really into it. I had a copy of it and I didn't want to only listen to it in the car. So I read the rest of it while walking the dog back and forth in the back parking lot. Fitz learned to trust me. And I learned that reading with the leash in my hand and a dog by my side was a decent enough way to get through books.

First time I told my wife I would not read and walk ever again: if not the day I was hit by a car, then the day after. I might have waited with such an important declaration.

First time I broke my promise: a few months later. The siren song of the book was too strong. But even though I was not following my promise, I was still only walking and reading on sidewalks.

First time I broke that rule, where I read books while walking the dog and there was no sidewalk: five years after the accident, just a few months ago.

First time I admitted that I might not have learned anything from the time the car hit me: right about now.

4

"The Girl, the Goldwatch and Everything," by John McDonald. It was a rare science fiction novel by one of the great masters of detective fiction. I read a few of his books, but never this one. I always wanted to read it. You see, I saw the TV movie when I was a kid. It was one of my favorite things I ever watched.

It was a strange TV movie in that it was aired as two one hour episodes. It was a mini-series, if a mini-series was just a two hour movie. It starred Robert Hayes, the guy from Airplane!, and Pam Dawber, from Mork and Mindy. I was one of the many pre-teen kids who had such a crush on Pam Dawber. It was not a torrid crush, I was a pretty innocent ten year old, but I could imagine holding her hand like I really meant it.

In this movie, she had a wicked streak about her. The character from Mork and Mindy didn't know about sex, but this Pam Dawber seemed to have an expanded repertoire. It was not a naughty movie, but I was sure to watch it by myself, away from the judging eyes of my family.

The plot was of a hapless young man who inherited his uncle's gold watch. He discovers that it is not an ordinary watch. When it is manipulated in a certain way, time stops for a minute. He can walk around in this frozen time. Everyone else cannot move, but he can do what he wants. That seems to be pulling silly pranks on people and winning money at the casino. There are people after him and his watch. He meets a woman, the girl, and they run off together, with the watch and all the time in the world.

I really loved this movie. I would try to get my friends to act it out on the playground during recess. They weren't too interested, because they hadn't seen it

I think I liked it a little more than other wish fulfillment flicks because I noticed that it was based on a book. Sure, it is a nonsensical juvenile men's sex fantasy (see all the books in the world and no one can stop you because everyone is frozen) but it has to have some class about it, because it was based on a book.

"Based on a novel by" in the credits of any movie was an excuse to be as dumb as any other movie. It was based on a book, so it is inherently classy.

I think I already wanted to be a novelist, so finding out that something I watched on TV was based on a book was a reason to believe in it. A book was written, I'm on board. I never bothered to read the books that the movies were based on. Just knowing that there was a book was good enough for me.

Interestingly, I never once tried to find the book. There was a book called, "The Girl, the Gold Watch and Everything" and that was ample justification for me enjoying a movie with Pam Dawber in it. Like I really needed an excuse to like a Pam Dawber movie.

5

Why do I read while walking?

Because it's the all around exercise.

Because words on paper love to strut their stuff in the daylight.

Because books should not be stuck away in stuffy rooms.

Because you become one of those weird characters in the neighborhood that everyone talks about. Ain't it fun to be a conversation piece?

6

One of the reasons I do not read while walking is to get interesting book suggestions from people walking by. I have had people tell me I should be reading Stephen King. I should be reading Dan Brown. I should be reading something good for me. I don't know why, but several people have stopped me to tell me I NEED to read, When Breath Becomes Air. I always say thank you and that I will put it on my list.

As if I need to be reading what they tell me.

Recently, I was kind of a jerk. A man, walking his dog, saw me and asked what I was reading? I looked at the book and answered truthfully, "A novel by Cesar AIra, an avant garde Argentinian writer." He took this in and thought on it. He said, "Oh," and continued on his walk..

There was no reason to be that pretentious, but it was what I happened to be reading. And one wonders why there is a strong anti-literacy streak in our society. Maybe it's because of high falutin assholes like myself.

7

For years, there is a guy on a porch that can't figure out why I read and walk. He will shout out, "What are you reading?" On the days when I am not reading and just walking the dog he might comment, "What, nothing good to read today." I tend to smile and wave.

His porch was one of the ones we visited for a Halloween. My son went up and said what he had to say and got his candy. The guy looked at me and said, "I need to know what is so important about your books that you have to read them walking."

His wife elbowed him. "Let it be. Halloween." My son and I thanked them and went on to the next door where candy was awaiting.

8

In April of 2015, I was excited because my son was going up to his grandparents in New Hampshire. Is that wrong to say? That I was happy my son was going away? Well, sort of bad. But don't we all need quiet and the chance to not focus on a six and a half year old. I mean, I can see plays with a six and a half year old, but there are occasions when I do not want to have see a hip, modern day version of Goldilocks. And books and movies that are not animated. I love all these things, but a pause from them is a lovely thing.

The plan was to have him spend time with his cousins up in New Hampshire and I would be able to read and walk. This is true. This was the plan. I was going to find a couple good books that would be perfect with walking the dog. Yes. This really was my objective. I was going to take the dog for long walks and I was going to read a book almost every day.

This was a brilliant plan. I would walk many miles and get in shape. (Yeah, this was my weight loss plan, walking with the dog while reading a book) I would finally get to read some of the books in the house. And the dog. The dog likes going for walks. The dog approves of this whole endeavor. Ask him.

My wife was going to be away for the first half of the week, but after that we planned going to some museums. We always took our son to museums, but that could be a hassle. Children have little patience with staring at pictures on the wall. To be fair, most adults have little patience for the same things. On the Thursday of the vacation week, the plan was to go into Hartford because the Athenaeum was having a large show about Coney Island. Go with me here. This is exciting stuff.

So this is it. Walking the dog. Reading books. Seeing art. Oh. And writing. I was in the middle of a long writing project that I was putting out as a blog and I was behind on the entries. I had much to write about.

(Okay, I should explain what the writing project was, because it does come up later in this story. I had gotten into my head that it would be interesting to go into every bar or restaurant in the city of Worcester, Massachusetts and have a gin and tonic. Then I would write about it. I was sure it wouldn't take that long. I mean, how many bars could there be in the second largest city in New England? I was now at the 107th bar that I went to and wrote about. The weekend that I dropped off my son in New Hampshire and started my vacation I went around the city and hit six or seven bars. This was not fun. This was work. This was writing. I had a readership, dammit. A good amount of people read the blog every week and I was getting invitations from newspapers to talk about my feelings about bars. So in addition to reading and walking, there was a good deal of writing I needed to get caught up with. In writing about the bars, I think I was behind by ten places. This was not a good thing, because my notes were always scanty and I had been drinking while at the bars, so my memory was shaky. I needed to get those essays out. Like I said, this will show up later.)

Walking around was not a crazy idea for a week off that year. It was one of the snowiest winters ever. In Massachusetts, we had over 100 inches of snow. We were having snow days well into April. This part of the year, near the end of April, might have been one of the first weeks of the year where the lawns were not holding onto snow, ice and slush. There was ground to see. And that was a joy. The idea that we can take long walks, the dog and I, was such a novelty. Of course I was going to take long walks. And of course I was going to bring a book along.

9

Why do I read while walking?

Because I have too many books in the house not to.

I was a man in his mid-forties who fancied himself a writer. And to be a writer, you have to read. That's what everyone said. Actually, I think I wanted to be a writer because I was already in love with reading. Maybe not reading as much as a love of stories. I wanted stories all the time. And I wanted to be surrounded by the stories.

And I loved buying books. I probably love buying the books more than I love reading them. I liked getting multiple books at a store and then bringing them home and opening up the bag. I would be surprised by the books all over. Even though I had purchased them just a few hours before. Look at this one. Look at that one. Where did this weird one come from?

Needless to say, I have accumulated books like barnacles on the skin of a giant whale. Every now and again I make the feeble attempt of divesting myself of some of the books. I know I will never read that novel again. Why keep it on a shelf? Every few years, I might bundle up fifty or so and donate them. But that never is enough. The population boom of books in my house far out weights the occasional culling of the herd.

And my wife is a writer as well. She was also starting the long process of getting her doctorate in literature. To that end, she required many books. There are bookshelves in every room of the house. But that doesn't suffice. Books are stacked on the wall by my bed in case I want to read before sleep. There are books by bookshelves, the unlikely number who could not find a space in the cozy confines. Books on chairs. In the corner of the stairwell landing. Holy shit. There are a lot of books.

A wonderful thing.

To walk around the house, I am constantly reminded that I should stop all the crap I'm doing and read something!

I have more books than I have days in a life.

So I walk the dog two times a day. On nice days, those walks are two miles long. Our dog was full of energy, the only way to get him to a nice calm state (or an approximation of calm) was a long walk.

Here is the thing about me and a long walk with a dog (two long walks a day), I can get a wee bit bored. A wee bit restless. I might as well do something.

I have books about the house.

I can read while walking the dog.

I am not doing it because I want to read more than walk the dog.

I am doing it because of the book explosion crisis in our house. If I don't read during this time, then the house will collapse from the weight of all those unread volumes.

And that is so much bullshit.

Because if that was true, I wouldn't have been going to Gibson's books on one of the days of April vacation for the sole purpose of buying a few new books that would be chosen to be read while walking.

10

What's the right kind of book to read while walking?

This is a ridiculous question. One that I have given a lot of thought to over the years.

The book itself should not be big. Hardback books are a bad idea. They are bulky to hold and the damned dustjacket gets in the way. How many times have I put the book down to clean up after the dog, and picked it back up to discover a few grass stains and a couple more rips to the cover? With that in mind, library books are not recommended. Hell, I will read library books, but then I am that asshole who ruins it for the next person. I'm a slightly frowned upon citizen.

I think the best kinds to read while walking are old style paperbacks, the kind that are easy to slip into a back pocket if the need for hands comes up.

When walking and reading, there is a part of you that is paying attention to the surroundings, so it is wise not to have a seriously difficult book. I am not a fan of small type in most circumstances. But when you are walking up and down the uneven sidewalks, tiny lines of text can be a pain in the ass to follow.

And I prefer short books. There is a sense of accomplishment if I can finish an entire book with just a few long walks. Now, that will never happen with a heavy Stephen King book. Also, small books are ideal for these idyls, because books can be weighty. You try holding up a seven hundred page book for an hour and a half while walking and not feel slightly weary. Books should not weigh you down, man.

For me, the perfect physical book is a short, one hundred to two hundred page book, that can fit in a pocket and has wide margins and a comfortably sized font. That's not a hard and fast rule. There are times I am jonesing to continue with a book. The dog beckons and I take this unwieldy book with me. The quality of the words always outweighs the package they are housed in.

Best to read early in the morning or near the evening. It is difficult to read the words when the sun is shining directly on the page. I don't have the best eyes to begin with and squinting while reading is not a good look, or a good way to avoid massive headaches later in the day. This is not a fun thing to admit, but I have bad eyesight and small print is beyond me at this point. Having good daylight helps in getting those letters to stay still and present themselves the right way on the page. Sooner rather than later, I will be that guy going to the Large Print section of the library. Of course those are large cumbersome books which are no fun to read while walking or even sitting at home, resting in a chair.

11

I remember buying the book The Girl, the Gold Watch and Everything very clearly. It was an exciting moment. It was a Saturday. It was the first day of the spring vacation. I work in schools, so I get the same time off as my son.

The plan was to have him spend a week with his grandparents and cousins up in New Hampshire. The way this was done is that we would meet at a halfway point, which usually was Concord, New Hampshire. We did the exchange at the Panera Bread parking lot. I hugged my son and told him I would miss him, because I certainly would.

As soon as they were gone, I put my nefarious plan in action. Instead of turning around and heading back to Worcester County, I made the turns to put me into downtown Concord.

The year before, my wife introduced me to what I think is my favorite bookstore in the world, Gibson's. They have been in business for over a hundred years. Their selection is wonderful. They had the typical books you would want to find at a bookshop, but they had so much more. It wasn't that they have a half million books, they do not. It is just that they select the books so well. They have the books I have needed even though I didn't know they existed. There have been several times when I wandered through their shelves and saw a book and instantly was convinced it needed to be mine.

We should all have bookstores in our lives like that.

I must pause to consider the fact that there are some people who are not as manic about books as I am. I am married to one, and that's a good thing. She might be more obsessive with buying books than me, which is kind of hard to imagine. Our son is being raised by two book nuts. His room is a labyrinth of book piles. If you pick the right path, you might find his bed, or the exit out. Some visitors are still missing in the maze of books.

I bring this all up because if you are not obsessed with books, then it might be hard for you to understand what you are reading. There is a need to own these things. Not just read them, though that is important. Having the object in your hand. Finding the right place for the book in the house. Or losing track of it and finding it years later and embracing the book like it was a long lost companion. That is the love of books I have. It is a need. A growing desire. I can stop anytime I want. I really can.

If you don't understand that, then you will be the one watching me walk the dog and read a book and wonder, not incorrectly, that I am fucking nuts. I will apologize quietly to you, hope you can figure out some of this compulsion and movie along with the story. We are still not at the car accident and we need to move along.

So, I went to Gibson's by myself. I didn't have to watch after a child, which is fun, but a six year old doesn't want to be around the literary criticism section of the store. That reader wants to be around the Star Wars Jedi Academy books, and quite rightly. This was such a treat for me. I could wander and take my time.

But after an hour, I was getting frustrated. I was looking for the right book and was not able to find it. What was the right book? Who the hell knows. I got it in my head that I wanted a book to walk with. I had the dog to walk and nice weather. I needed to get a new walking with the dog book. As I said earlier, I was being a terrible book owner, spurning all the previously purchased books for this, the next new thing. Always have the eye for the pretty new ingenue, I suppose.

What made a good reading while walking the dog book? Like any judge coming up against obscene material, I would know it when I saw it. But it was now an hour in and I wasn't finding it. It was elusive. It was making me work.

Then, on the fifth time through the store, I went through the science fiction section. If I have any complaints about Gibson's, it's that the shelves are close and the lighting is not sufficient (for me at least). Only in this time through it, did I see the book. There it was. The Girl, the Gold Watch, and Everything.

It all came back to me. The flood of it. The movie. Pam Dawber. Stopping time and frolicing. All that joy of watching something slightly subversive brushed up against me and I took the book off the shelf. I weighed it in my hand. It was a little longer than I was planning. It had some heft. But the rush of recognition hit me and I knew that this was it. This was the book I needed to read while walking the dog through this lazy week. It was a certainty.

I ask this question to myself often, though I know it is ridiculous and not helpful in the least. But still, I ask. If I had purchased another book instead of this one, would I have been hit by a car? All the South American butterflies who subscribe to chaos theory sit on the sidelines and laugh. They don't answer the question, because there is no real question to respond to.

We are the events that occurred. Only those things. We are allowed wishful thinking, but only in the late hours, with the lights out, and the pain throbbing in a wounded body.

12

Why read books while walking?

We moved to our neighborhood in 2009. I don't think I walked around it too much. I did take walks, but not too much. It was nice enough. Parts were a little run down, but it was nice enough.

In 2014, when we got the dog, I was forced to learn my town, whether I wanted to or not. I was very aware of where I was walking and because Fitz was very energetic and curious, I focused on the ground in front of me. If there was an old, dirty, piece of thrown away food or even a discarded chips bag, that dog zeroed in on it.

This made me notice the detritus on the ground. I heard conversations from porches. I was aware in a way that I might not have been before on my walks.

And that's how I noticed the tossed away dime bag. The syringes. The nip bottles. The occasional and inexplicable piece of clothing by the curb, absorbing dirty runoff water like a misbegotten sponge. That's when I noticed the permanent products of desperation.

I heard fights from windows. I watched old women struggle to get their groceries up the rickety stairs. One early morning, there was a man on a bike riding from one house to another, staying for a few moments and then moving on. Delivering something.

And I started reading more often. My eyes on the page. Interpreting another land. Another world. I read of worlds that were not perfect or ideal, but they were at least not the one I trod on. If I focus on the story on the page, I don't even hear what's around. They say books transport you. Maybe they don't do that exactly, but they certainly make the one you live in, unfocused and leached of color. Like walking through an old, blurry sepia snapshot.

One time, while walking the dog, and reading a book, a police car stopped by me. Rolling down his window, he said he sees me walking around all the time and maybe he saw this kid he's looking for. He described him down to the backpack. I shrugged a negative response, unhelpful and dumb. I said, "Sorry. I didn't see anyone. I was." I stopped and pointed at the book in my hand. The cop shook his head and rolled his eyes and continued his search.

Why read books while reading?

Because you will be forgiven for your ignorance of the world.

13

There is something to be said for the act of walking in aiding to the reading experience. Your muscles are moving. Your mind is working harder than when just reading at home. You are paying attention to the things around you (you hope) and what the book is telling you.

Your brain remembers the book more vividly when you put in effort. You are walking and exercising those major leg muscles. You are keeping your back straight and your arms stiff. If it is a heavy book (and that might have been a bad choice of reading material) then you are really stressing those biceps.

I am not promising you a Charles Atlas body from reading and walking. This is not dynamic tension at work. This is just reading on the go.

This is a way to use your body to increase your memory. Walking offers a jolt to the brain. The catalyst that makes the reading stick. Some of the best moments of reading have been outside in the sun with a dog to my side and a book resting in my palm.

There is a book called Spark that talks about how even the minimum amount of physical exercise will increase a student's ability to learn. I love how there is a book that excuses my poor behavior. I have to read and walk. Science tells me to.

I am not in great shape. But I can only imagine what type of bilious amorphous blob I would be without my love of reading and walking.

14

We are well into this little book and we haven't reached the big event. We still have not made it to the car hitting me. Where the hell is the accident? This is taking forever.

I am as surprised as you. I thought we would get there pages ago. It was such a brief event, and yet, the distance to it seems to expand as in a Fun House hallway.

Maybe this is the sign of the writer not wanting to get to the place he needs to be. Maybe i am putting it off. Maybe I am sparing myself. I don't know if this was a traumatic event, but it is a large landmark in my history.

I have a lot of words at my disposal and I have built them around this morning like a wall against the waves. If I look at the landscape of your personal history, I am sure I will find it pockmarked with sea walls and hastily constructed battlements.

Ah fuck it.

Let's get it over with.

15

It is Thursday at 7AM. My wife is home from her trip. My son is away in New Hampshire. I have only 50 pages to go in the book I am reading, The Girl, the Gold Watch, and Everything. I am excited because if I have a long enough walk with the dog, I will be able to finish it this morning. The book is good. I like it's companionship, as much as I like having the dog walking to my left.

My wife is asleep. I stretch and get dressed. We are going to Hartford today, to see the Coney Island exhibit at the art museum. I am excited. I still remember going there as a kid with my grandmother. I remember more, the tales my mother had of going to the Steeplechase when she was a kid. And how great Nathan's hot dogs were. I am hoping to have these memories mingle with what I will see on the museum's walls. But right now. I am looking forward to finishing the book I'm reading.

Finishing a book is a mostly sweet pleasure. There is a tang of disappointment to the good ones. It is the sour realization that there is no more. The joy is done. The comedy is over. Finishing a book is another step up on the long mountain climb. The peak is in the clouds.

I don't like when I finish a book halfway through a walk. I have nothing else to enrapture me. I am left with a weight on my hand. Something to be lent out or stored away on a shelf. But the story has been taken from it and all that remains is the mile walk back home.

If I can arrange it, I love completing a book right when I get back to the house. That's the way a finish should happen. There are times I will circle round the block a few times to get to the last page as I reach my driveway. Fifty pages, I should be able to swing it this morning.

As I walk down the stairs, I hear the thump thump thump of the dog's tail. He is, no doubt, lying on his side. When he hears me in the morning, his tail starts slapping the wood floor. His metronome greeting to me. Fitz makes the beat that says, "Don't dawdle. Just get the leash already. I've been dying for this moment." Nothing makes me happier than hearing the thump of the tail when I approach. It is a lot to live up to.

The leash is on. The poop bags are in my pocket. I have my keys. I don't have my phone. It's all the way upstairs. I could go up and get it. Nah. I don't need it. It's just a walk around the neighborhood. I pick up the book. Yep. Fifty pages more. Figure that is about two miles of walking. The dog is now impatient to get outside and he nudges my leash hand with his snout.

We are outside, Fitzgibbons and myself. I go down North Main and hang a left onto Crescent. After I pass the Balmer School, it turns into Swift road. This is a long arc of a road. The houses are nice here. This is where I take my son trick or treating in October. We know where the good candy resides.

When Swift ends, I take a left onto Goldwaithe. In a half mile, it will meet up with North Main and a quarter mile more on that, I will be home. I think it is long enough. Fitz would disagree, he would want more walk. This is why I don't ask him. I am into the book. I am getting a little worried. How can they resolve everything still happening in just the thirty or so pages remaining. I hope that he doesn't rush it.

There are no sidewalks on Goldwaithe. It is a little twisty. Now that spring has decided to show up, the trees and foliage have greened up and the visibility has lessened. I walk on the edge of the road. My feet are on that line of asphalt and grass. Fitz is always on the grass. He prefers being on someone else's property over the public sidewalks and streets. There is a rebel in him. He lingers on stray smells. He pulls his attention away from our forward momentum. I continue walking and he complies. We are both walking forward. I turn pages when I need to. I am getting to the end. The big conclusion.

And the car hits me.

16

I will say this again.

The dog was fine.

He still is great.

I should also let you know what kind of dog he is. I am sure you want to know what he looks like. You are rooting for him in the story, you should have a picture of him.

He is a black lab mix. He is damned cute. He is fifty pounds of shedding fur. After we took him to the dog trainer, he doesn't bark at anyone. He is not stand-offish. He is always in your business.

My friend Gary, who dog sits sometimes, calls Fitz the world's worst guard dog. If he sees you at the door, he will run up and allow you to pet him. When we are walking, he and I, and we pass someone on the sidewalk, he will lean into them. Some folk tense up when he does this, but all he wants is for them to pet him. I am constantly saying to people crossing our path, "Friendly. He's friendly. So damn friendly."

I think we were lucky to get such a dog from animal rescue. Sure, he needed a little help and training. But primarily, he is a good being. He doesn't want to hurt. He only wants the best for you. And to his mind, the best for you is to pet him and give him treats. He knows what you need.

He was so confused when I was sprawled down in a mess of limbs on the side of the road.

17

I hear, more than feel, the thud. I am in the air. I am thinking thoughts. I realize that I have the leash in my hand. I somehow deduce that I didn't run into a wall but a car. I calculate that I will be hitting the ground soon. And I am right. It hurts more than the car did.

I am silent and still.

I take in air to my lungs in a shallow attempt of a normal act. And it works. There is breath.

I exhale.

My focus is on the ground. I am mostly on packed dirt. I feel something wet and furry push on my temple.

The dog is checking on me.

"I got hit by a car," I inform him. He takes it in stride.

I think I should be in pain. I am feeling numb.

A car pulls to the curb a few yards from me. She has a dent on her passenger side door and the rear view mirror has been mostly ripped off. I did that? I ripped off the mirror with my incredibly strong body?

A young woman gets out of the car. She is upset. More upset than me at this moment. I'm just hanging out here on the ground. Chilling. Biding my time.

She asks if I'm alright. I tell her I'm good. I try to sit up. I don't remember how.

She walks over to me. I yell at her to stay where she is. I swear at her. I know the moment I tell her to stay the fuck back that I will always regret it. I shouldn't be swearing at her. She didn't want to hit someone this morning. This isn't Deathrace 2000. Her day is ruined as well. Her plans have been upended too.

Someone calls the police. An older man, who lives in the house I just passed, comes by. Checks on me.

I stand up to prove that I am okay. I sit down again.

"You got hit pretty hard," he tells me. He looks and sees a book five or six feet from me. "There's a book there."

"That's mine."

The woman is by her car, crying. The older man is telling me that he wished I didn't get hit by a car right in front of his house because he and his wife were planning to pick up a new dog this very week. "She wants to get it. But I wasn't sure about it because walking a dog on this road always seemed like a bad idea. Then you get hit right here. Now. I don't know if we should get one."

"Dogs are great," I say. "You should get one."

The police arrive. He checks on me. The dog leans into him and waits to be patted.

The police officer goes over and talks to the driver. She is a teacher at a Catholic school who was heading to work. She had a little bit of a morning glare, turned the bend and hit me. Like that.

The cop asks if I saw it. I tell him I was reading a book.

The older man says after the police officer goes back to his car, "You shouldn't have told him that."

"Tell him what?"

"That you were reading. I see you all the time walking here. You are always with your head in a book. You shouldn't have told him that."

"Why?"

"Because then it's your fault."

"But I was on the side of the road. I wasn't in the middle of the road. I don't think I was in the middle of the road."

"You reading a book makes it your fault."

"But I got hit by a car," I say.

"While reading," he points out. He doesn't ask me how the book was. I could tell him that it's pretty good. We don't speak much now. The ambulance arrives.

They tell me I got banged up. I figured that out by myself. They confer with the police officer. They say they would like to take me to the hospital. I ask them what will happen to the dog if I go in the ambulance.

The police officer tells me he can drop the dog at my house. It's only a little bit away.

I have a vision of my wife awakening from the pounding of a door. I can see her going downstairs to be greeted by a policeman holding our dog with me nowhere in sight.

I don't want to do that to her. I think of calling her but rediscover that I left my phone at home.

I say I will go home. The EMTs say it is better if I go with them. I tell him I want to go home with my dog. They have me sign a form that I was going home against medical advice. I shook the older man's hand. I get in the back seat of the police car slowly, gingerly.

Fitz bounds in right next to me and rests his head on my lap. He keeps it there for the entirety of the short trip.

When I get home, I feed the dog, because that's what you do after walking the dog. Walking up the stairs take much longer than I expect. I wake my wife up and tell her I got hit by a car. But I am okay.

She thinks I am kidding.

"No," I say in between exhausted breaths, "I got hit by a car when I was walking Fitz."

"How's the dog?" she asks.

"He's fine."

18

That day, I stayed in a chair and found it harder and harder to get up and around. My muscles seized on me. We didn't go to the museum. We didn't do much. We went to the doctor and got some pain medicine. Eventually, I had to go for an MRI and be in physical therapy. I was old road. I was gone from anything like walking. The dog nestled by my chair, waiting to start our walks again.

That day, a reporter got in touch with me out of the blue. She had heard of my Gin and Tonics Across Worcester blog and wanted to go out with me to bars and have gin and tonics. I looked at my unmoving body and laughed. Like that was going to happen. I asked her to send me questions instead and she did within an hour. I sort of remember answering her questions. I was going to be in the paper. And all I wanted to do was not feel so beat up. When the article came out, I was shocked by what I replied. Did I really say that? I had no clear memory of anything I said.

The book, The Girl, the Gold Watch and Everything made it home. I don't know how exactly. But there it was, next to me in the chair. I opened up the book. I found my place easily. It was the page with ground dirt. I finished it. I was disappointed. The story was rushed. I wonder would i have been more satisfied with all these conclusions if i hadn't been hit by a car.

The next day, the young woman's insurance agency started calling me several times a day. They wanted my side of the story. They wanted to know if I really was reading. I told them the truth. They wanted to come over to my house and have me sign some papers and maybe they might even give me some money for my trouble.

That was the clue that I was in over my head. I contacted some lawyers. They took care of it from there. The lawyer was clear with me, I should not have been reading. I was being reckless, in a legal way. He told me I shouldn't have told the insurance people I was reading. "What?" I asked. "Should I have lied?" He told me that of course I should never lie. But still, it would have been great if no one knew about me reading.

After about nine months I was given a check. It wasn't a lot. The lawyer said it would have been so much more without the reading. Isn't that always the way?

19

At work, it was kind of a joke. Dave got hit while reading a book. One person said, "I was just like Stephen King." No. Not like Stephen King. He almost died. I was just dinged.

A few days after the accident, I tried to put my best foot forward and run the poetry reading I do every week. When I walked into the bar, everyone asked me what was wrong. I told them. One regular nodded, "Yeah, I got hit by a car. It sucked." Another regular said, "Yeah, I got hit by a car twice on the same day. Can you believe it?" I thought about it and said, "No, I can't believe it."

The strangest response was from the office manager for the department i worked in. She was angry at me. "How could you be reading while walking the dog. I don't care if you were just reading a book and got hit by a car. That would have been fine. But you were with the dog. You were ignoring your dog. Walking a dog is a sacred time. You have to give all your attention to him. You have to be with him and him only. Not reading a book. I know I shouldn't say this but you deserved what you got."

20

I didn't know what the dog felt about it until about eight months later. I was walking him one cold morning. I slipped on some ice. After a few moments of flailing about like a drunken ice skater, I fell down hard. Nothing terrible, but I did wind up sprawled out on the sidewalk. I felt like an idiot.

As soon as I was down, Fitz was right on me. He put his nose to my face. He nudged me several times. "I'm okay," I told him, like I was expecting him to understand. He was afraid, I decided. He didn't like seeing me fall down. I wrapped my arms around him and hugged that smelly, shedding, wonderful dog. "You're a good guy," I said. "I'm alright. You're a good guy."

I was never a person who wanted a dog. I was wrong. At that moment, still seated on the icey walk, I knew how wrong I was.

21

Why not audiobooks? Why don't you listen to audiobooks while walking the dog? Wouldn't that be easier? Smarter? Safer?

I think the answer to all those questions is yes. Yes all the way.

And yet, I don't.

I have listened to books on tape (that shows how old I am), some on Audible and books on YouTube, while walking. But when it's time to start walking I tend to not get my device and headphones. I tend to pick up one of the many books on the desk and head off.

I think I prefer the technology of picking up a book rather than prepping the technology to have something read at me. Does this make me a luddite? Yeah. Kinda.

Books are easier. Books are friendly. Books walk with me. They do not whisper in my ear.

Now, don't get me wrong. I love audiobooks. The long commute I have every day to work is mitigated, if not enlivened, by all the books I listen to. Hell, I once went to see George Guidall speak at a library because he is one of my favorite audiobook readers. He has read over a thousand audiobooks and I am such a fan. The way he read Neal Gaiman's American Gods makes it the best way to experience the work. George Guidall is one of my two favorite audiobook readers. I have favorites.

But reading and walking is much more vibrant than reading and listening. More active. More life threatening.

There was a time I walked and listened to books every day. I was taking a year off from teaching by selling health insurance in downtown Worcester. (When I took a break from education, I really went as far as I could go) We were given an hour for lunch. I soon discovered how boring an hour lunch was.

Quickly it turned into a set routine. I would eat at my desk a half hour before my lunch hour. Then I would put on an old walkman (which was an analog IPod) and the latest cassette of whichever book I got from the library.

And then for fifty five minutes a day, I wandered around Worcester while listening to literature. I remember walking through the blasted streets of Main South with the noon time prostitutes and the any time junkies, clogging up the street corners while hearing what the narrator of A Tree Grows in Brooklyn went through and how things really haven't changed much. Or in the rainy days of winter, I would walk the dying downtown mall while Oscar Wilde's The Picture of Dorian Grey was read to me. As I watched store after store turn to papered over windows, I got to hear the list of the riches Dorian Grey collected. The dissonance from what I saw and what I heard was an amazing sensation. Those are two of my favorite times with a book.

But for the most part, there is an inherent muscle pleasure of holding the book while reading. The act of walking with a book held up is an important part to the way I want to have a story told to me. I wish I could just listen to the book. But I can't. I want to be an accessory to the act.

22

I wish I could say I learned my lesson. I wish I could say that I never walked and read again. But we know that's not true. I already told earlier in the book. And even if I didn't tell you, you probably would have guessed it. Some guys never learn.

It was quite some time before I read while walking. The first reason was, my body hurt and i had to seriously concentrate on walking the dog. Every step up and down the sidewalk took a good amount of mental navigation.

Then I was wrapped in paranoia. My lawyer told me I should not read while walking the dog. If I am found doing it, there will be no money. There was hardly any money anyway, but it did get me questioning the others I saw on my walks. Were they spies for the insurance company? Were they out to prove me bad?

Eventually, I gave into the thing I really loved doing. It isn't boredom. It is the simple truth that I just like walking and reading. It is the act. I might say I was bored while walking the pooch and needed something to occupy my mind, but no. I like doing it.

But I had a rule. No more walking and reading on roads without sidewalks. It is a good rule. I think it is one to live by.

And I wish I could say I followed it to the letter. But recently, the dog and I have been taking longer walks. This is the time of the Covid-19 lock down where I have been working from home. What else is there to do but walk the dog? And read books? I have found myself being bolder than I have been. There has been a time or two where I have walked in an area without any sidewalk. And I didn't stop reading.

It's not a good idea. I will no doubt not do that again. Yeah. No doubt.

23

For this long weekend that I gave myself for writing this book, I went to Brattleboro, Vermont. The plan was to hole up and be in a town I like to write in. It's the end of the weekend and I have reached the second to last chapter, so I guess the location was good for me.

But a long weekend isn't about writing. A fella has to eat. A fella has to procrastinate by watching videos on YouTube. A fella has to justify all that eating and procrastinating by taking a long walk. On the Saturday of my time here, I decided to head North on Route 30. I walked for about four miles and then turned around.

I brought along two books. As soon as I was on 30 and saw that the side of the road had really wide breakdown-bike lanes I felt comfortable to read. As much as I portray myself as a reckless reader, I do pay attention to where I am walking with my book. Sure, I might run into a parked car or a lamp post every now and then, but I still try to be careful in my fashion. Five years after the accident, I will still jump when a car rushes close by me. Perhaps that's a good thing.

I took out a children's novel I purchased a while ago, Knee Knock Rise by Natalie Babbitt. She wrote Tuck Everlasting and I recently discovered some of her books and think she is an amazing author. It is only a hundred pages, which is perfect to read on a lazy walk. The story was beautifully told. I was enraptured. A town has a monster that lives on the mountain above them. No one has ever seen it, but they hear it groan and howl when it rains. The town has become a tourist attraction because of the monster. But is it real? The book dealt with faith and the need to believe even if empirical evidence tells you otherwise. I finished it after three miles. It was wonderful. There are certain books classified for children that should be read by everyone. This walk was a success because a fine book was read.

I started the second book I brought. It was a small volume called Hero by Lee Childs. He is a thriller writer and the essay said it was his thoughts on the idea of the hero. It sounded good. Even though the book was less than 80 pages, I couldn't get through it. After forty pages, he was still talking about the anthropological groundings of storytelling. He also had a chapter about the naming of the narcotic heroin, which comes from the word heroic.

The sun was warming the road and the cars were becoming more frequent. The trucks blasted by, but not so close to make me twitch.

I only had thirty pages to go and about two more miles before I made it back to downtown. I could finish it. Just to say I read it. But the world is finite and there are so many good books I haven't read. Why should I bother with one I don't like? I am one to stop reading a book, but it is always with a sense of regret. I always wonder if I missed something great. Something hidden away in the final page.

I put the book back in my pocket and took out my phone. I have the Kindle app on my phone and will read when I don't have a book nearby. I will read and walk with my phone sometimes. I prefer books though. Reading on a phone doesn't feel as pleasant to my body.

I have a strange library of e-books on my phone. Today, I read a book about vampire films I had never gotten around to finishing. It was filled with descriptions of films I probably will never even attempt to see. But it was words to be read. A day with the body walking in the sun and a story to be told

I walked for eight miles and had a wonderful morning. I went to a coffee shop and had an egg sandwich. I continued reading while I ate. Can't stop doing a good thing. I realized my right knee was sore. It gets that way after long walks. Wear and tear and a slightly busted body.

24

This is not a manifesto. I am not looking for recruits in the Reading-Walking Army. I am simply telling you of a pleasure in my life that is also an annoying peculiarity.

The body wants to move. We walk. We want to enjoy our time with the dog. He is happy to tag along. We also want to be told a good story. We want to know new things that might be stored in the book. So we read and walk. We know it's not the best of ideas. A quirk. A shortcoming. A silly notion.

The book in my hand. The story in my mind. The dog keeping pace by my side. Rain is coming and we pick up our pace.

Finished Sunday June 28, 2020 10:15 AM

Vulture! Vultures Everywhere!

Begun July 10, 2020 1PM

"I beg of you monsieur, watch yourself. Be on guard. This place is full of vultures. Vultures everywhere" -Casablanca

"On a morning from a Bogart movie, in a country where they turn back time, you go strolling through the crowd like Peter Lorre, contemplating a crime" -Al Stewart

"Are you telling me you'd be happier with Victor Lazlo then with Humphry Bogart?" - When Harry Met Sally.

"Only the Roman roads lead into the open. Only the most ancient traces lead anywhere. Where is the top of the pass here? And it's only there that my country, the land of storytelling, begins." -Wings of Desire

"I don't like champagne glasses. They remind me of operettas." - Remembrance

"Welcome to the Latchis. Casablanca is in theater one" - Said to me by an usher on June 26, 2020.

"With the coming of the second world war, many eyes in imprisoned Europe turned hopefully or desperately toward the freedom of the Americas. Lisbon became the great embarkation point. Not everybody could get to Lisbon directly. So a tortuous, roundabout refugee trail sprung up. Paris to Marseilles. Cross the Mediteranean to Oran. Then by train or auto or foot across the rim of Africa to Casablanca in French Morocco. Here the fortunate ones, through money or influence or luck might obtain exit visas and scurry to Lisbon. And from Lisbon to the New World. But the others wait in Casablanca. And wait. And wait. And wait." -Casablanca

Casablanca: Minute 2. One of the things not mentioned often about the film, Casablanca, is that the beginning is an unpleasant info dump. That disembodied narration lasts over a minute, which only feels like a long time when you are in a movie. A minute long speech is a huge amount of celluloid real estate. I suppose they needed people to understand the world they were creating, but must we have the Voice of God explain it all to us?

"It still smells the same, only dustier." - Wings of Desire.

I go to Brattleboro every few months to write. I have been doing this for several years. This year, with the Covid-19 lock down, I have not been there. But boy, did I ever need it. Staying at home and trying to work over Zoom was hard. Having the family also go through the hardships of isolation was another level of stress.

When Vermont started to open up, I made a reservation to be there. I love the artistic temperament of the town. I love the Latchis Hotel, where I stay. It is in downtown and convenient to everything. The Latchis was built in the 30s and has a wonderful Art Deco feel. There is a grand old movie house attached. It has been a very good place for me to focus on writing, and also a place to recharge my batteries with art and music and theater.

There was no music and theater at all. Half the stores were still closed. The restaurants were all take-out. I had no other choice but to stay in the hotel and write. I found out the art museum was open. I walked around the galleries, in my mask, for an hour. I did not realize all the little joys I missed. Like going to a museum. Like seeing a movie.

I love movies. And I love the idea of seeing movies at the Latchis, because I could stumble down from my hotel room in my socks and in two minutes be watching a movie. One of the four screens still has much of the art and murals of when it was a movie palace. I have seen great movies here and a few that I wondered what I was doing wasting my time. Of course, the answer was that there is nothing wrong with wasting time with a movie. No movie is bad when you are wasting time in the right way.

Bloodshot, starring Vin Diesel, is a bad movie though. And it should not be the last movie you go to before everything is shot down due to pandemic.

Casablanca: Minute 3. Still slow and plodding. The next two minutes are only slightly better, because someone is shot dead. That always adds a little spice. We see a large backlot full of day players establish that two men are being looked for by the authorities because they have stolen important documents and the French police are rounding up all the disreputable types they can find and one gets nervous and runs away and is shot. His dead body holds a clue of where the missing documents might be.

We now have a scene of the pickpocket with an older British couple. The pickpocket is only in the movie for two brief scenes, but we will linger on him. Who cares about Humphrey Bogart or Peter Lorre contemplating a crime. We have the man on the button, making a living. Doing what needs to be done. We will follow him for as much as we can. He hides in the shadows. He doesn't let his presence be known.

Because we are in a land of exposition, the pick pocket is also so infected. He doesn't speak in sentences but in synopsis. He tells the British couple and ourselves what the hell we're watching. "Two German couriers were found murdered in the desert, the unoccupied desert, and this is the customary round-up of refugees, liberals and of course beautiful young girls for Mr. Renault, the Prefect of Police. Unfortunately along with these unhappy refugees, the scum of Europe has gravitated to Casablanca and some of them have been waiting years for a visa. I beg of you monsieur, watch yourself. Be on guard. This place is full of vultures. Vultures everywhere. Everywhere."

Of course, the British man cannot find his wallet. He doesn't say it was stolen. Why would he think that it was stolen? The world is a kind place for those of privilege. You never have to check after your valuables. They are always safe. "How silly of me. I left my wallet in the hotel." We find ways to survive through the simple act of lying to ourselves.

"Now the virus that we're talking about having to do. You know a lot of people think that goes away in April. With the heat. As the heat comes in. Typically that will go away in April." - President Trump on February 10, 2020

"How silly of me. I left my wallet in the hotel."

"Yes, the theater is playing movies this weekend. They are starting small. Two movies this weekend. They're going to show Selma, because that's a good one about civil justice and we are all thinking about that. And they decided to play Casablanca, because it's the perfect movie to be playing in an old movie palace. If you are going to go back to seeing a movie in a theater, it should be a classic in a classic place." Jonathan, that manager of the Latchis Hotel, which is attached to the Latchis Theater.

I love Casablanca. I was raised to love it. My mother loves World War 2 movies, and this and the Enemy Below are her two favorites. But Casablanca is more well loved, so it was on TV a few times a year. It was a treat when it was on Channel 11. My mother would make it a big thing to watch it.

Besides bing a movie my mother likes, I love it for the dialogue, the speed and the way I cry at a particular scene. Everytime that scene shows up, I cry. I have given up being embarrassed by that and embrace the idea that a movie has the power to control my emotions at will.

The amazing thing about the pickpocket scene is that we never see the crime. The pickpocket puts his hand on the man's chest. He moves his arm around slightly. But our eyes are on the magician and we can't see how the disappearance has happened. It could have been just an embrace. A moment of contact between others. How much safer and less crime ridden the world would have been with social distancing.

The pickpocket was played by Curt Bois. He was a Jewish German who fled the Nazis. He was a child performer in Berlin. He sang songs in a high lilting voice.

If you go to YouTube you can hear some of Curt Bois's recordings from 1930, when Berlin was wonderful and not about to burn. He sings like Joel Grey in Cabaret. It is funny singing. It is ironic. Even with a knowledge of German, it cannot be truly translated for us to understand.

Six minutes into the movie and we finally meet characters we will see again. Characters that move the plot forward. Major Strasser of the SS. He is a mean son of a bitch. And Captain Renault, the corrupt French police officer. He's everyone's favorite corrupt cop. He's bad and oh so lovable.

A month after the killing of George Floyd by police in Minnesota, there is still protesting around the country. Some might not find the police so lovable.

I read somewhere that they softened Renault before the film's release. They were concerned that Renault was sleeping with young women under the pretence of giving them an exit visa. This is confusing to me, because it is obvious from what is said and what is shown that Renault is doing that very thing. Where was the softening? How bad was it before they fixed the problem?

The movie started at seven. I got food from the Food Co-Op and ate in my hotel room. I was doing well with my writing project and I was celebrating with a break for food and a movie. I even got a sweet desert, a raspberry bar. On eating it, I realized something was wrong. It was delicious, just the texture tasted like something. I checked the label and there it was, walnuts. I am mildly allergic to them and very allergic to black walnuts. My attitude is to avoid all kinds of walnuts. My throat felt the same, but that did not stop me from panicking a little.

With only a few minutes before the movie, I walked briskly back to the Food Co-Op and picked up a bottle of Children's Benadryl. I drank a quarter of it and put it in my pocket. By the time the movie was well underway, I was well under too. It was a jaunty, loopy version of Casablanca. As if all the actors wore slightly bigger shoes and dug for the laughs a little harder than usual.

Nightclub scenes in old movies always sadden me. I see everyone sipping amazing cocktails, dressed impeccably while listening to a man at a piano. People smoke cigarettes and have witty conversations. I have never been to such a mythical place. I wonder if it was all created by Hollywood. The night club as a figment of a black and white past. They say that Rick's club was based on the Hotel El Minzah in Tangiers. But even if the table cloths were pristine and white, there would always be a tingling sensation that it is not as good as the ones in the movies.

Nine minutes into the movie and we at least see Humphrey Bogart. He has been waiting in the wings for his big entrance. Actually, he was probably drinking in his trailer. We see him annoyed, authorizing funds to keep the Cafe running. He smokes his cigarette like the locks are on the door and no one will get in. He plays chess with himself.

Rick does not allow a man for Deutsche Bank into the private room. It is a brave act that does not hold much value so distant in the past.

On entering the movie lobby, I paid my nine dollars. I paused for a second, expecting the usher to tell me the rules of the road. When I was to wear my mask, when I could take it off. How close can people sit to each other. I was sure that the rote speech was coming my way. I received none. I was on my own.

Casablanca: MInute 10. Bogart to Peter Lorre, "I don't mind a parasite, but I object to a cut rate one."

"On a morning from a Bogart movie, in a country where they turn back time, you go strolling through the crowd like Peter Lorre, contemplating a crime" Al Stewart in Year of the Cat

The story of the song Year of the Cat was that Al Stewart had the music for some time, but did not know what to do with it. He loved the chord progression but had no story that might meld with the music. No words to fill up the bones.

Al Stewart saw a book his girlfriend had showing the Vietnamese Astrological Years. That's how it became the Year of the Cat. But he said when he sat down to write, a Humphry Bogart movie was on. Thus, all art is explained as happenstance and desperation.

I am pretty sure that Peter Lorre is captured and killed in Casablanca before he has any opportunity to walk through a crowd that makes him contemplate crime. I don't remember any long guilty strolls in the Maltese Falcon. Maybe he did that guilty walk all the time and was so good at it. He was lost in the crowd, avoiding the notice of police.

The movie I think of when I hear that line of the crowd and crime, is his early German film M. In that he is a child killer who skulks about the streets of Berlin whistling. He is always contemplating crime. But I am pretty sure that is not the inspiration to the song lyric. No one wants to be thought of as that character. No one wants to run down the streets with such fear, such desire, such desperation. No one wants to wear that Peter Lorre suit. No one wants to be wrapped up in the heavy overcoat and sung about.

Casablanca: Minute 11. "Rick, do you know what this is? Something that even you have never seen. Letters of Transit signed by General De Gaulle. Cannot be rescinded, not even questioned."

Yes, I know this is just the MacGuffin. The Letters of Transit is just something created to move the plot along. Peter Lorre will die and Bogart will have them and everyone will try to get them from him, but let's be fair. The Letters of Transit makes no sense. The big thing is they were signed by General De Gaulle and cannot be questioned. Why? De Gaulle had fought against the Germans and soon fled to England. Why would something he signed have any power in a corrupt government under the sway of Germany? I know. Don't worry about it. The movie will happen and you will have a good time. The Letters of Transit are important because there wouldn't be a movie without them.

After buying my ticket, I look at my phone, it is 7 and I don't want to miss any of the movie. This is a dumb thing to worry about, for I have seen this movie countless times. Doesn't matter. I hate missing a minute of the movie. I might not be focused when I am at the movie, but I want the full amount of film I paid for. Whether I like it or not. Whether I follow it at all. But there is nothing to worry about. The movie I know has not yet begun.

Casablanca: Minute 14. Ferrari wants to buy the Cafe. Then he offers to buy Sam the piano player. Rick replies, "I don't buy or sell human beings." Ferrari speaks like a modern American wading through dangerous political waters with aplomb, "Too bad, that's Casablanca's leading commodity. Refugees alone we can make a fortune." I once complained to a friend that I could not understand why the current administration is doing what it is doing and my friend told me to, "Follow the money. Always ask who is going to benefit financially from it. Everything they do and say is about money." Ferrari would have to agree with a sense of pride.

There is someone wandering through this movie. Curt Bois. He left Germany because of the Nazis. He made it to New York. He liked the strip clubs. Maybe they reminded him of the clubs he played back in the Weimar Republic.

"I don't like champagne glasses. They remind me of operettas." -Curt Buis from the documentary Remembrance.

What's wrong with Billy Crystal? Is he being dense? His platonic love interest, Meg Ryan, tells him over the phone that she is watching Casablanca on TV and he asks what channel. This is nuts. Why would he have to ask what channel to watch Casablanca? If that movie played in New York in the 1970s and 80s, it was on channel 11. That was the channel that played Casablanca several times a year. It was an event. It would not have been a surprise that Casablanca was on channel 11 and Billy Crystal would be aware. They advertised before they aired it, because it was a big deal when Casablanca was on. Was he just playing dumb? How could he not know? And that is why I cannot believe in the movie When Harry Met Sally.

Casablanca: Minute 17. This is my favorite line from this or any other movie. I love it. I use versions of it all the time, much to the chagrin of my family. Renault asks, "What in heaven's name brought you to Casablanca?" Rick says, "My health. I came to Casablanca for the waters." Louis is puzzled and says, "Waters? What waters? We are in the desert." Rick says, "I was misinformed."

Many times I will say I went somewhere or did something for a ridiculous reason. When someone looks at me with confusion I will say, "I was misinformed."

Curt Bois was in America for fifteen years. He was in scores of movies. He had a few lines and left. He was the fussy European. A minute here in this film. A minute there in the next. If you addup all his Hollywood screen time, how much of a movie would he have? Would it be a full film? A short subject? Enough to entertain? Enough for a career?

There is a famous picture of the singer Debbie Harry looking all punk glamorous. She is wearing a baseball t-shirt that features a picture of a bird and it says "Vultures." You can purchase copies of this t-shirt online. You can be cool like Debbie Harry for a decent fee and the cost of shipping.

"When I arrived in New York, in 1835, I mean 1935, there were striptease clubs on 42nd Street. It was marvelous. I'd be there from 11AM to 11 PM. I was just thrilled. All the time in one or the other. If anyone wanted me, they'd tell him, check the striptease joints. The most famous was Billy Minsky's place." -Curt Bois from the 1980 documentary, Remembrance.

Casablanca: Minute 20. Renault tells Karl, the head waiter, to give Major Strassa the good table. Karl says, "I have already given him the best. Knowing that he is German and will take it anyway."

I also say "I blame society," a lot. It's from the movie Repo Man. I love that line almost as much as adore the line, "I was misinformed." For some reason, my family hates how often I say, "I blame society," as if I really do.

Casablanca: Minute 21. Peter Lorre is gone. Out of the picture. He has been taken away and not to be seen again. He is one of the top billed actors in the movie and he is out after being on screen for five minutes. Life means very little in Casablanca. So does screen time. You will have to make the most of your scant moments on the screen. You have to be memorable as you are dragged away by the police.

I am replaying that moment in the end of June when i watched the movie at the Latchis, but I am watching it again while writing this. I have a good memory, but not a great one. I thought we had the DVD at home. I love this movie. Why wouldn't I have it home? I spent a half hour going through all the places DVDs are kept in the living room. It is hard to remember a time when we bought and hoarded these things. I could not find it. How could I not own it Casablanca? Even if I would not think to watch it on a random night, I always thought of myself as the kind of guy that owned a copy of Casablanca.

Many of the DVDs we owned are in the original plastic. Never to be opened. Things to be stored for the perfect time to watch, if there ever is such a thing. It is Schrodinger's DVD Box. As long as it is never opened, it is the movie you thought it was and it is also all others all at the same time. Every DVD is Casablanca as long as you don't open it to find out.

Casablanca: MInute 24. Major Strasser reads from a dossier about Rick's history. Rick takes it from him and looks at a random page. He asks, "Are my eyes really brown." I mention this line because it was the favorite line of an old roommate of mine, Bob. Whenever we watched the movie in our rundown apartment in Cape Cod, he would pause the VHS tape when this scene arrived and said the line before Bogart could. "I love that line," he would announce.

There are so many great lines in this movie. I don't know why. Maybe I have been conditioned to think they are great. But no. The movie is an amazing collection of axioms. I can guarantee that I will not mention your favorite line, your favorite part. There is too much to pick. Your favorites are probably better than mine.

Walking into the auditorium to watch the movie, I see a few groups of people. The auditorium is huge, maybe about four or five hundred seats. In the days of the old movie palaces, that was only a tiny theater. And this was bigger in the past, parts of it have been divided into small screens. I am wearing my mask. I sit down in the front of the theater. I take my mask off and look behind me. There are some people with masks still on and a few with masks off. The couple nearest me wears their masks. Their eyes are visible and they are shooting daggers at me. They are pissed at me. I put my mask back on.

Casablanca: Minute 25. Bogart gets up from the table of vipers. "Excuse me gentleman, your business is politics. Mine is running a saloon." I am bothered by how short sighted that comment is. Running a saloon is politics. My friend is going back to the bar he works at, now that Massachusetts is slowly opening up. He doesn't know if he wants to deal with people and the way they feel about masks. Should he tell them that the law requires the wearing of masks before they sit at their table? Should he get into a partisan debate so that he can make them whiskey sours and pour them beer? When the world teeters on its normal axis, every place is politics.

Minute 25 is also the minute of the movie where Ingrid Bergman walks in. And generations of movie goers, maybe some right here in this theater, hold their breath at the unexpected beauty walking in through the front door like the rest of us slobs do.

My old Cape Cod roommate, Bob, also informed me of why Paul Henreid was famous. "I don't know who that is, so how famous can he be?" I said. "He plays Victor Lazlo, he's famous because he was the first guy in romantic movies to put two cigarettes in his mouth and light both and give one to the lady he has his eye on." I said, "That doesn't sound romantic, that sounds kind of creepy." Bob said, "He's known for that move. Back then, that was a big slick move." I'm sure I said, "If you say so," and went back to the movie.

Casablanca: Minute 27. I take in my breath when I hear it. It comes from the lips of the most beautiful woman in the world. She asks, "Captain, the boy who's playing the piano. Somewhere I've seen him." And suddenly she is not as beautiful. The boy she is referring to is Dooley Wilson, who was around fifty five years of age when he made this film. He was paid five hundred dollars a week for the movie, which was pretty low for the time.

In the lobby of the Latchis are locally made posters with quotes from African American people. There are quotes from James Baldwin, Maya Angelou, Martin Luthor King, Jr. In the other theater, the film Selma is playing. It has been a month since a man named George Floyd was killed by the police. It was not the first death of a black man by police. There have already been other deaths to fill out the crooked list since his murder. People want change. People don't want anyone, even the wonderfully vintage Ingrid Bergman, to call anyone a boy.

"I love America more than any other country in this world, and exactly for this reason, I insist on the right to criticize her perpetually." - James Baldwin. From a poster placed in the lobby of the Latchis Hotel.

Casablanca: Minute 30. An exotic woman sings a song Tango Della Rose. She has a high operatic voice. This was Corrina Mura. She was the step-mother to the macabre writer and illustrator, Edward Gorey. There must be a story there. There is always a story when someone sings in a Cafe.

Casablanca: Minute 34. "I remember every detail. The Germans wore gray. You wore blue."

Years ago, I visited Portland, Oregon. I was a young man without a care in the world. I wanted to go to Powell's City of Books and to get there I passed through some rough spots with porn shops and people crumbled down by the sides of buildings. As I was walking, my eyes on the prize of a good bookstore, a car pulled into a parking spot right where I just walked past and blasted his horn. What the hell? I turned to look at what he was on about and when I turned my body back,

I noticed that someone had his hand in my pocket. The pickpocket said nothing as he detached from me and walked quickly into the first available store. He didn't even warn me about vultures. The car pulled back into traffic. I was amazed. Someone thought it worth their time and effort to help me keep my wallet. I should have been horrified that I almost had my wallet taken, but was instead elated that some stranger cared enough to help. I soon found Powell's and was quickly overwhelmed by all the books waiting for me.

Casablanca: Minute 37. Drunk Rick says, "Sam, it's December, 1941 in Casablanca. What time is it in New York?" Sam says, "My watch stopped."

No one knows what time it is anymore. People will call up friends to ask what day it is. I didn't know it was Tuesday. You want to look like the smartest person in a pandemic? Know what day it is. Know what time it is. Refuse to let things blend into each other. Don't let time break any more then it has.

Curt Bois returned to Germany in 1950. At first, he went back to East Germany. After seven years he went to West Germany for more acting opportunities. This was before the Berlin Wall was erected. Even still, walking from one Germany to another could not have been easy. That is a piece of sleight of hand that is not as simple as picking a pocket or taking a necklace.

Humphrey Bogart was shorter than Ingrid Bergman. To look taller than the woman he loves, they had him stand on boxes. They made her sit a lot. Of course she was sitting all the time. Being that tall in such a diminutive world is exhausting.

One of the great joys of my life is going to the movies with my son. It's a thing we have done since he was three. It's nice that he is eleven and I can take him to movies I might want to see. But even if it is a dumb Alvin and the Chipmunks movie, I love the companionship. I love the idea that he might adore going to the movies as much as I do.

The last movie we saw together before the theaters shut down was Blood Shot. It is a Vin Diesel superhero movie. My son had not heard of it, but I figured it was a comic book movie. How bad could it be?

Casablanca: Minute 43. Sam, Rick and Ilsa attempt to drink all the champagne before the Nazis come into Paris. "This ought to take the sting out of being occupied."

We are not occupied, but are told to stay in our homes and not get close to anyone. The virus. The invisible has us cowering, looking for microbe troops marching down the boulevards. Only the essential stores are open. Liquor stores are considered essential and they all are doing fine essential business. It takes the sting out of it. Or at least, that's we say while sit in front of the last piano in Paris.

They say that Humphrey Bogart improvised the line "Here's looking at you." Others say this writer or that writer came up with it. Others point to an older Bogart movie, Midnight, where he said the same line. Only the line itself knows, and the line ain't telling.

I am getting lost in the movie. I am finding connections that the filmmakers had nothing to do with.

It turned out the movie Blood Shot was terrible. My son was trying valiantly to find something to like about the movie. I was not paying attention. I was texting with a distraught friend.

Casablanca: Minute 44. Rick asks Ilsa where was she ten years ago and she says she was getting braces off her teeth. Her perfect teeth. She asks him the same thing and he says, "I was looking for a job." He knows exactly the moment. The time there was nothing to do. The time that everyone looked and no one found. It was not an activity, it was a way of life.

One of the things everyone says about Casablanca is that the chemistry between Bogart and Berman is amazing. And it is. They seemed to be like two people who like each other. What a rare and astounding skill. To make people think that the blood is boiling and the heart is pounding. Even when they probably weren't.

"I don't even understand this character. It's amazing how little I know about this part. Maybe we'll discover during the shoot. I'll get a good costume, that's half the battle." Peter Falk in Wings of Desire.

Curt Bois was in Wings of Desire, 1987. It was his last movie. He was Homer, the storyteller. The old man in the library with a world of knowledge and the dread knowledge that no one will want to hear. The angels stand by his shoulder and listen to his thoughts. He musings. They dip into his mind like a thief in the night. Pickpocket.

I don't wear the mask for the whole movie. I let the ties unravel and let it slowly slip off my face. Maybe I helped it along a little. I didn't look behind me. I didn't want to know if the nearby couple were looking at the movie or at me, the terrible bringer of disease. I know I should have kept the mask on. But I was happier having it off. I didn't know what that says about me.

Casablanca: Minute 50. "Tell me. Who was it you left me for? Was it Lazlo or was there others in between, or aren't you the kind to tell?"

I am surprised by a movie I have seen countless times. Sitting in the fifth row of the Latchis theater, I suddenly notice that the first half of the movie takes place all in one night. I know that the movie started as an unproduced play, so the three act structure is there. But I never knew that everything happens all at once. From Lorre getting captured to Bergman showing up to Bogart having a long drunken flashback sequence. All one night. The big moments happen in an instant.

I don't understand the allure of movie palaces. I can see the murals and the beautiful columns that line the auditorium. But for what? What elegance can we see in the dark? What beauty is allowed for us to compliment when we are focused on the movie before us?

Before he was in Wings of Desire, Curt Bois was the subject of a documentary. Two younger German actors interviewed two older German actors. One was Curt Bois who had to leave during the war but returned to a career. The other actor stayed and was the darling of the Nazi era stage. His later career had not been as successful.

Casablanca: Minute 55. People who have seen this movie too many times will start to notice the refugees Jan and Annina. Annina is young and fresh faced. They have shown up several times in the movie looking desperate. Here, Ferrari is telling her that maybe she can come to an agreement with Renault, the Prefect of Police. In others words, sex for a visa. There is more with her and her man, but I am taken with how well enmeshed they have been in the movie. They are the countless masses who will now be shoved to center stage. Briefly. But they will be there in the spotlight.

I remember once going to the world's greatest movie palace, Radio City Music Hall. I was seven or eight and this was one of the last years they did a whole floor show before showing a movie. I picked the movie. It was the premiere of Matilda. This was a film about a boxing kangaroo that was so disliked it was never released after it was shown in places like Radio City. It was a bad movie even for a kid like me. But it was what I wanted to see and I was so annoyed about how big and fancy the place was. And then they had dancing and a kickline show before I could finally see my boxing kangaroo movie. Why were they going all out with all this opulence for a boy from the midwest who only wants to see his kangaroo movie? Wasn't it just a bit of overkill?

Casablanca: Minute 57. "You will not find a treasure like this is all Morocco, mademoiselle. Only 700 francs. Ah, the lady is a friend of Rick's. For the friends of Rick, we have a small discount. Did I say 700 francs? You can have for 200. And for special friends of Rick, we have a special discount. 100 francs. Ah, I have some tablecloths. Some napkins. Please, one minute."

Ingrid Bergman is wearing a hat like a large inverted fruit bowl. This is what she took on her flight out of Europe, a misshapen frisbee?

Instead of paying attention to the movie Blood Shot, I was responding to a friend. WIth the Corona-Virus shutting things down, he was laid off. He was worried about the future and sounding depressed and dire. I texted him throughout the movie, all while telling my son that the movie isn't that bad.

Ferrari calls himself "the leader of all illegal activity in Casablanca." Really? All illegal activity. What about jaywalking, do you lead that? Is every person perpetrating indecent exposure iin your debt as well?

If you watch Casablanca on Amazon Prime you can find out all the actors in every scene and read fascinating trivia. At the moment in the Blue Parrot Cafe, they inform us that there is a goof with the liquor bottles. They all have United States tax stamps on the bottles. I have watched this movie a lot, but not to the point of noticing liquor tax stamps. And if I did, would I want to admit it to people?

Ferrari ends conversations in the best possible way. He picks up a fly swatter and slams it on the table. That is the way to let people know that you are done with their conversation. That is the way to let people know what you think of them.

My son was pissed at me. "You weren't watching the movie. You were on your phone. I wanted you to watch the movie with me. And the movie was bad."

Casablanca has been praised for its brilliant screenplay. It is a wonderfully told story. But how the hell did that happen. It was based on an unproduced play. Then Aeneas MacKenzie and Wally Kline worked on the screenplay. Then the Epstein brothers worked on it. Then they brought Howard Koch on to have it be more political. Koch and Epsteins were both writing dueling scenes as the movie was being shot. They didn't even know how it was going to end. Casey Robinson came on as well to help focus the movie. And yet, the movie holds as a cohesive whole. All the cooks made only one dish.

Casablanca: Minute 61. The pickpocket returns. Or. It is only the second time we are allowed to notice him.

At the bar at Rick's, he is chatting to a man. The pickpocket removes the wallet. We see it this time. "I have to warn you sir. I beseech you. This is a dangerous place, full of vultures. Vultures everywhere.

Thanks for everything. Good bye sir. It has been a pleasure to meet you."

The pickpocket bumps into Carl, the head waiter. The pickpocket apologizes and walks on. Carl is panicked. He pats his pockets to make sure that the thief didn't steal from the establishment. He is relieved. He hasn't gone broke today.

In both times we see the pickpocket he uses the same term, vultures everywhere. It's his trademark. It's the one thing people remember about him when they report the robbery to the police. "He was short. He was polite. He said something about, I don't remember, something about buzzards, buzzards all over the place." Shouldn't a thief who doesn't want to be noticed not use a catchphrase? People will know, the minute you hear a guy talking about vultures, hold on to your possessions. Maybe the police call him the Vulture. Maybe they call him the Buzzard.

Who am I kidding? Everyone knows who the pickpocket is. He pays a sum to Ferrari, because as he already told us, he is the leader of all illegal activity. The pickpocket also pays off the police. It makes things safer that way. But how it eats into his bottom line. For every dollar he steals, he only keeps forty cents. It's a tough world and the wallets seem to be getting thinner.

Curt Bois gets the spotlight he might not want in the only version of the Documentary, Remembrance, available. It is a 90 minute film but the only copy I can find is as an extra on the Wings of Desire DVD. They compiled only the parts with Curt Bois. The other actor and all the other parts have been left out. Like we only want to hear from Curt Bois. In the documentary, there was a contrast shown between the two old actors, I suppose. But here. We get only one. We are not privy to the long story. We eschew the details and only look at the one thing the producers of the DVD think we might like to know. We might like to see.

Casablanca: Minute 65. The young girl, Annina, asks Rick what kind of a man is Captain Renault and he says, "Just like any other man, only more so." And once again, we are in the world of creepy cop abusing his power. But Claude Rains plays him so slyly and he helps Rick in the end. We should forgive him all his indiscretions. We should just accept the rot and decay.

"You want my advice? Go back to Bulgaria."

"You want my advice? Go back to Mexico."

"You want my advice? Go back to Honduras."

"You want my advice? Go back to your home and self-quarantine until I tell you to stop."

I attempted to explain to my son why I was not paying attention to the Blood Shot movie. I had to text my friend. I was worried about him. My son understood, but then said, "When we are at a movie, we should pay attention. Even with bad movies."

Casablanca: Minute 72. The Germans in the bar are singing some German song. It is very martial. It is nothing like the fun patter songs Curt Bois sang when he was knocking them dead in the cabarets. This is a beer hall song that lets people know who is allowed in the hall and who is not. The refugees cower at the song. Lazlo goes over to the band and tells them to play La Marseillaise. The band hesitates. They look to Rick. Rick nods.

Humphrey Bogart nods. Not Rick. Rick knows exactly what he is agreeing to when he allows the band to play La Marseillaise. Rick knows this is a sign of partisanship and forgotten loyalty. Rick is smart like that. Bogart just nods. He does not know why he is nodding. He could be just saying hello to an old friend who waved from across the room. He might nod to get the kink out of his neck. Bogart nods because that's what he was told to do.

The story goes, the film's director told Bogart that he had an easy day. All he had to do was nod. Just nod once. Look serious too. That helps with the nod. We don't want a happy, ginning nod. After you nod, you can go home. We got this. That is what Bogart did. He nodded. He allowed the band to play. Bogart didn't know this. He didn't know how brave he was being. He was probably already planning what he was going to do with his time off. Golf? A good book?

To see the movie, you would swear that Bogart knew exactly what he was doing with that nod. And he did. He did know. Nod. And then go home. That's how patriots are made.

I cry everytime the La Marseillaise scene shows up. In the Latchis Theater I am surprised that the movie is suddenly unfocused. But then it comes to me, I always cry at the scene and my eyes are watering up.

I can't help crying at this scene in the movie. It seems so easy to show your patriotism with a song. All you need is a catchy melody and a desire to do the right thing and the world will be better. They shout out, Viva La France when they are done. But France is still alive, just not the France they want. Maybe they will never get their France back, though it still lives. Maybe I am crying for that. Maybe I am crying for grand useless gestures. Maybe I cry because this is the place, the scene, that I permit myself to weep.

The Amazon Prime movie trivia for Casablanca tells me something I did not know. That the La Marseillaise scene is taken and adapted from a 1937 French movie, The Grand Illusion. I know of the movie. I never have seen it.

There are so many great movies I have not even heard of, let alone seen. There are classics to explore and experience. But yet, I watch the same movie over and over, and I cry at the same scene over and over.

I watched the La Marseilles scene from Grand Illusion. It was quite moving. The scene shows a drag show being performed in a camp for French prisoners during World War 1. The French prisoners have made themselves all Fab-U-Lous singing and dancing. Someone from back stage announces that they got word the French army took a fort from the Germans. One man, in drag, pulls off his wig and has the band play La Marseilles. The performers take off their wigs and sing. Soon, all the prisoners in the audience have stood and are singing. There is a brief shot of the German guards looking on. It is a powerful moment and one cannot blame the makers of Casablanca for dipping into the well to get some of the magic.

In Wings of Desire, there are camera shots that fly past the devastation of the bombs. Not recent bombs. But grandfather's bombs. The buildings that were blasted and made worthless still standing derelict forty years later. A grand monument for the scope of destruction.

Now, after seeing both La Marseillais scenes, I have to give it up to Casablanca. I know this was never a contest. This should not be a contest. There should not be winner and a loser.. But, I'm sorry. Casablanca is better. For no other reason then I have watched it since I was eight or nine and the Grand Illusion is new to me. Only today I have watched scenes preserved in the transient amber of YouTube. It is all too new to me to give up a half century of belief. Can I just say that I love them both very much, and they are such good boys.

We have a president now that yells at football players for taking a knee in protest to police brutality. The people who took the knee during the playing of the national anthem said very clearly that this was a protest to police violence. The president told the country that the football players are wrong, in both their act and the words. They are not protesting the police, but are just being disrespectful to the flag. To the national anthem. The president said the football players are being disrespectful to the soldiers and troops. The act of taking a knee is not about what they said it was, but what one man with a large megaphone said it was to be. The core of the problem is not the issue. It is the super-imposed flag. It is the desperately sung anthem. The song that is supposed to meld us into one. The president said that the issue of violence against the people is not the issue, but it is those who are willing to take a knee and say that the problem is still here.

Vultures. Vultures everywhere.

Casablanca: Minute 73. Yvonne is saved. She sings La Marseillaise and is not longer deluded. She shouts out Viva La France louder than anyone else. Or maybe that's just the sound mixing. She was a bar girl. She was with Rick for a spell. She was drinking pretty hard. Who can blame her. She was fraternizing with German soldiers and lost her way. Now that we all sung La Marseillaise, everything is right again. She will kill the German soldier in his sleep. She will shave her head and join the resistance. She will mine the trade roads with bombs. She will explode with emancipation.

Casablanca: MInute 75. "My dear mademoiselle, perhaps you have already observed that in Casablanca human life is cheap."

Sitting in the Latchis Theater, watching an old movie, finding it easy to not think of how cheap life can be. The president does not mention the virus anymore. He does not mention the death. Over a 120,000 died from the virus in the last four months. No one needs to mention the value of life here.

Casablanca: Minute 77. "Ilsa, when I was in a concentration camp, were you lonely in Paris?"

I tell my son he should watch Casablanca with me. He says, "okay sure" and quickly leaves the room. Am I to force him to watch the things I think will be good for him?

Casablanca: Minute 79. Can someone explain how femme fatales or spurned women show up in apartments or offices that are impossible to get to. Rick has a club that has been closed by the police. He is locked up. There is a curfew. He has a private office that is called that because it is private, no one can get in. But there is Ilsa waiting for him. She tells him she got in from the stairs in the street. How is that possible? Shouldn't the stairs from the street stop someone, anyone from getting in? Did she use the backstairs entrance that has a sign saying "To Private Office, Do Not Use?" Did she swing in through the window using mountain climbing gear? Did she walk on to the set as easy as pie after coming from make-up and wardrobe? All answers that will not be given. She looks so good in the shadow, does it matter how she achieved this impossible task?

Casablanca: Minute 80. "I wouldn't bring up Paris again, it's poor salesmanship."

I don't know if it's true, but I think this three and half months is the longest I have gone between seeing a movie in a theater. Going to the theater is always something I want to do. It is damned expensive, but I never want to give it up. This long stretch took away so much. Who knew movie going would be the thing to keep me sane.

"I used to go out a lot, but I don't do that now. I'm cured. Not one of these glasses please. I don't like champagne glasses. They remind me of operettas. The count of Luxembourg or Countess Maritza. And then you have to sing. Just a plain tumbler, that's fine." -Curt Boise from the documentary, Remembrance.

Casablanca: Minute 82. I am so impressed with the tears in Ingrid Berman's eyes as she pulls the gun on Bogart. Maybe it's this. This sense that it really is happening, or that it is the best piece of make believe ever, that makes this a movie to watch again and again. And write books about it, and bore people to death with it.

Casablanca: Minute 83. Let us say it, the way we see it. Rick and Ilsa do it. They kiss into a fadeout. Maybe its something we learn only from old movies, but the fade out while two people are kissing means only one thing. Sex is happening in the breath between that scene and the next. The longer the fade out, the steamier the sex is. It's just a language we used to learn. No one speaks this visual tongue anymore. We have to learn it like any unused language, like Latin or Yiddish.

"Are you telling me you'd be happier with Victor Lazlo then with Humphry Bogart?" When Harry Met Sally.

One of the things I have read about Casablanca said that they had to change the script to get rid of any sign of the two of them getting it on (that was the proper term from the Hayes Office). But it's right there. They kiss and the next scene is Bogart at the window smoking a cigarette. If they tried to get rid of any notion of the deed, they failed.

Casablanca: Minute 85. We had Ilsa being racist. And now we have her taking the role of the second class female "I don't know what's right any longer. You'll have to think for both of us. For all of us." Let the saloon keeper think for me. The saloon keeper knows best. The saloon keeper is so smart and sexy and plays chess. Let him move the pieces. Wait. She has more to say. "I wish I didn't love you so much." So romantic. So unhealthy.

"On a morning from a Bogart movie, in a country where they turn back time, you go strolling through the crowd like Peter Lorre, contemplating a crime" -Al Stewart

The song, The Year of the Cat, follows a young tourist who wanders off and meets an exotic local woman. He goes to her place and has sex. In the morning, he has missed his chance to leave with the other tourists, but is still feeling amorous toward the woman. He knows he will leave her, but not right now. Right now is fine enough. It is a movie and we are all Peter Lorre hoping Humphrey Bogart will be impressed by us at last.

Casablanca: Minute 87. "Do you wonder if it's worth all this?"

I sit in the theater and ask myself that very question. Is it worth all this? Is it worth wearing a mask while watching a movie you have already seen? You have to watch the old movies you have already seen because there are no other movies being released. Is it worth making sure no one walks near you? Is it worth the amount of stress wondering if you should wear the mask at this moment or not? Of if it is safe to sit in this specific chair or not? Is it worth all of this to see a movie?

Yes.

Seeing a movie in a big old theater is the greatest activity you can do while sitting in the dark. It is a joy. It is a pleasure. And now, I realize that it is also a privilege that I might not be awarded. I never thought going to the movies would turn into an honored event. One with fear and trepidation but a sense that it's worth it. And we can imagine that it is the same happy event it always was. It is not. It has changed.

This is not the most uncomfortable I have been in a theater. This is not the time I really feared being at the movies.

The most controversial movie in the late 80s was the Last Temptation of Christ. It seemed like a cool movie. Harvey Keitel was Judas. David Bowie was Pontius Pilot. Martin Scorcese makes a good film. And many Christian organizations were losing their minds over it. People were protesting the theaters it was showing at. Tommy wanted to see it bad. It was playing in two places in Manhattan and neither of us wanted to drive in and find parking. The third place it was at was in New Jersey. We went there. Tommy insisted we get there early, to make sure we got in. We arrived over an hour early. We started talking to one of the bored ushers. The usher was over this movie. "I am so sick of all the TV crews here all the time. And the protestors. And now someone is calling in with bomb threats. It's so boring." My eyes widened. Did he say bomb threats?

I spent the entire time watching Last Temptation of Christ in a panic. There were shouts and weird sounds from out in the lobby. I didn't know what they could be. Are those the typical sounds at this theater? I liked the movie. I thought it was pretty good for a bible flick. But was it the movie worth dying over? Is this the line in the sand film I would give my life for? I was petrified the entire length of the picture. And I never had a more exciting or memorable time at the movies.

I have seen Casablanca on the big screen before. It was in 2002 at the Bijou Cinema in Worcester. I was so excited to see it large and in my face. I am sure I loved it. I am sure I cried where I always cry. I am sure I left satisfied. But I do not remember anything more than that. There was no bomb threat to keep the recollection close to the surface of my memory. There were no protests going on outside. There was no virus floating about, waiting for a beachhead to stumble upon and invade.

Casablanca: Minute 89. "You're not very subtle, but you are effective."

I suddenly realize the one thing wrong with this moment of movie going: no snacks. Going to the movies is about getting over priced Milk Duds and a tub of stale popcorn. Movie food is it's own food group, and well deserved. But I didn't even think to buy anything for this. Would that be an imposition to the other people in the theater? Was I supposed to move my mask to the side, shove a fistfull of popcorn into my mouth and then put the mask back? No. It was easier to leave the candy alone. But something about that made the activity thinner. Not as rich. Not as salty.

Casablanca: Minute 91. RIck is selling his club to Ferrari. He tells Ferrari that Sam gets 25 percent of the profits. Ferrari says, "I happen to know that it is ten percent, but he's worth twenty five." Oh man. Again with the selling of the piano player. In the beginning, Rick said that he does not buy or sell people. Now he is abandoning his oldest friend and making sure his business rival pays him more. I know we are talking about salary, but it still feels like buying people.

"You know nothing about men like me!" Vin Diesel in Blood Shot.

Wings of Desire. Near the end. The angel has decided to be human. He lists all the things he will do when he is human. "First, I'll take a bath. Then, I'll get a shave, from a Turkish barber, if possible, who will also massage me down to my fingertips. Then I'll buy a newspaper and read it from headlines to horoscopes. On my first day, I'll have everyone wait on me. If someone wants something, they can ask the next guy." Is this the dream of an angel or the one of someone in quarantine?

Casablanca: Minute 94. Rick tells Renault that he has a gun pointed right at his heart. "That is my least vulnerable spot."

Samuel Johnson wrote an essay where he talked about a man who could understand the language of vultures. The essay translated the supposed conversation between a mother vulture and her children. " 'Man,' said the mother, 'is the only beast who kills that which he does not devour, and this quality makes him so much a benefactor to our species.' 'If men kill our prey and lay it in our way,' said the young one, 'what need shall we have of labouring for ourselves?' 'Because man will, sometimes,' replied the mother, 'remain for a long time quiet in his den. The old vultures will tell you when you are to watch his motions. When you see men in great numbers moving close together, like a flock of storks, you may conclude that they are hunting, and that you will soon revel in human blood.'"

One of my favorite scenes is when Renault is told to call the airport. Instead he calls Major Strasser. I love his character. He is bright and self serving. I am almost disappointed in him

for getting some patriotism and helping Rick out.

It has been months since my son and I have seen a movie. The last one was so bad. Will he want to see a movie with me? Will he trust me enough to pay attention to the movie? WIll he trust me again to pick a movie worthy of paying attention?

The airport. They were not allowed to shoot in a real airstrip because of the war, the filmmakers used a fake runway and a small cardboard plane. The plane was small, maybe ten feet at most. To pull off the flim flam, they filmed little people, dressed as airport workers, to give it the right scale. On the big screen, the illusion still works. There is nothing off about the airport mechanics. There is nothing off with the airplane ready to whisk you off to the promised land. It is not made of cardboard. It is made of gold.

Casablanca: Minute 96. The speech. The big romantic speech. It has things about maybe not today and maybe not tomorrow. It says something about a hill of beans, which makes me realize that I am hungry and I wish I had a hill of baked beans. Or popcorn.

The big romantic speech is great, and it's the big fireworks. But I love the little lines. The lines that make a character, that make a world. The tiny bits of wit and truth. The big romantic speech is a grand show piece, but all those little lines are what makes the altar for the showpiece to rest upon and be admired.

Casablanca: Minute 97. Ilsa: "I said I would never leave you." Rick: "And you never will." That's how you stay cool while being romantic. Like that.

The end of the movie. The plane gets away. Rick shoots Strasser. Renault tells his police to round up the usual suspects. Rick and Renault walk off into the foggy unknown. "This is the beginning of a beautiful friendship."

I don't believe that last line. I love it, but I don't believe it. I don't think either will survive for long. I think they are walking off into a war neither of them ever made. They say that they will make it to Brassaville. But we see them walk into the mist, who can ever be sure of the casualties when everything is obscured?

It is an ending that lies to itself.

And I love it.

Curt Bois walks away from us in the last moments of the movie WIngs of Desire. It is the last thought. It is his last movie. It will be his last line, as a voice over. As a thought that could be changed and re-recorded. But he is full of thoughts and wallets he took from others. "Tell me of the men, women and children who will look for me. Me. Their storyteller, their bard, their choirmaster, because they need me more than anything in the world. We have embarked."

This wis what going to the movies should be. A wonderful location. A killer movie. But I am by myself with no one to share it with. And there is no no-man's-land of dirty floors and stale popcorn to navigate around. I miss the specificity of the movie going experience.

At the last scene of the movie, I put my mask back on. I don't want to be seen with a mouth and nose.

With the lights on, I turn and look at the others in the theater. Half don't have their masks on. I am shocked that I am spending so much of my brain on thinking about mask etiquette.

The couple who looked at me with steely judgement still look at me the same way. Maybe it's just their thing.

Walking out, the night is humid. I don't feel Benydryl loopy anymore and decide to walk around Friday Night Brattleboro to see what is going on. It's nine o'clock and most of the town is deserted. The restaurants and bars are all dark.

If there are angels, they have large wings and circle about the sky looking for carion. They feast upon our private thoughts, our broken fears.

Walking through the crowd like Peter Lorre, contemplating a crime. No crowds. No crime. Just a line from a song I might not recall correctly.

I see only one or two homeless people, when usually there are ten or fifteen hanging about. I wonder where they are sheltering. What place will be the home they stay at? The endless refugees.

Passing the Stone Church, once a typical church, now a music venue, someone passing me brushes by me. It is odd to feel human contact rush by on a summer's night.

As soon as he passes me, my hand shoots down to my back pocket. I feel the contours of my wallet in its place and breathe relief.

Vultures. Vultures everywhere.

Completed July 13, 2020. 12:30 PM

Adrift on the Lost Channels: A Love Story of the 1970s

Begun on Saturday, November 14th, 2020 at 9am

1

Speed Racer

There was an ongoing plot. There was a forward motion to Speed Racer. It was not just his Mach 5 that barreled to the finish line at amazing rates. There was a complicated plot that had something to do with his lost brother, who turned out to be the mysterious Racer X. This moved forward. This was a driver of motion and interest.

Speed Racer was a cartoon from Japan that I did not see a lot of. I liked it. But I didn't watch it all the time. I am not sure, but I think it did not play in Illinois in the 1970s. I will be saying this a lot: I am not sure. I do not completely recall.

My memory of Speed Racer was watching it at my Grandmother's house. It was the only time I could see it. My grandparents lived in New York and we visited several times a year. My mother did not like living in Illinois. She lived in New York City for most of her life. Even when we moved to a house in New Jersey, Manhattan was only a fifteen minute drive or a walk down to the train station.

Now we lived in Naperville, Illinois, a suburb of Chicago. This was not anything my mother expected or signed up for. Well, she signed up for the marriage to my father and he was transferred to the Midwest. She moved, but she didn't have to like it. She was now compelled to wonder how a Jewish girl from Brooklyn would want to survive in Naperville.

To mitigate this, her mother flew in from New York often. Every few months, Grandma arrived with offerings of New York. She brought Jew food. It is hard to imagine that there was once a time that bagels were an exotic thing, but it was true. No one had seen such a strange creation before. It was foreign. It was delicious. It was bitter sweet. The taste of being in a place you don't want to be.

With those visits, we also went to New York. We stayed in Grandma's guess room at her apartment on Tahema Street. And we watched kid shows that I didn't know about in Illinois. New York was big and loud and filled with cartoons that never traveled to the middle of the country.

And this is how I remembered Speed Racer, King Kong (there was a cartoon show), and other shows. Speed Racer might have been on in Illinois, but maybe it was aired during the school day. Some channels did that. They played the cool cartoons at noon or at six in the morning. The TV Guide might whisper of wonders that I was too sleepy to partake of.

Speed Racer might have been the show I only saw when I was sick, and watching TV while wondering how long I could milk this cold and stay home for.

My memory has me watching Speed Racer sitting in my grandmother's second bedroom. There was a secret jolt in the viewing because I knew I would not be able to see this on a normal day. This was special. This was secret joy.

With a lot of these memories, they are boiled down to one recollection. It is a colorful, animated madeline that brings back a world. For me, Speed Racer was that incredible theme song. "Go Speed Racer, Go!" I still sing it to myself when stuck in impossible traffic and I have the faith that if I sing about driving fast, I will be doing it in real life.

There were other scattered images of car tires dancing on the edge of cliffs and some of the wonderfully goofy hi-jinks of Chim Chim the monkey. And was Chim Chim also one of the pit crew mechanics?

I have no idea how many episodes of Speed Racer I watched. Perhaps a handful from start to finish. That's how I remember kids watching television. Afternoon kid shows were designed to pecked at. The show was on, but then you had to run to the kitchen. There was a phone message for your mother that you said you wrote it down, but you probably didn't. You ran out to see if anyone was playing nearby, and then ran back to see if the show was getting good. You might be building legos or reading a comic or searching the corners of the suburban house for stray money or copies of Dad's Playboys or an LP with dirty words in it. And then, when inertia spun down, you might see how the program is going. What terrible straights have the heroes gotten themselves into? Maybe you will watch them get out of the mess, but you trusted they would survive whether you witnessed it or not.

And that is how we watched television as kids, all while navigating the no-man's land terrain of the time between school and when dinner appeared on the table.

I liked the show. But even though it was a special program that I only watched in New York, on foreign televisions that I could not claim as mine, Speed Racer was too popular for me to claim as my own.

I did not realize it, but I craved the unknown, the unpopular. I wanted a show to be mine and mine alone. The perfect television show was one that no one but me watched. It was not a lonely way to see shows. It was perfect. It was personal.

2

Prince Planet

It's funny that the second chapter of this book is another Japanese animated show. There will be a few other anime, and a lot more of live action Japanese kaiju shows. It is odd to see me write about anime, because as an adult, I have always said that I don't like anime.

I guess it goes without saying that I wander in a world where adults talk about anime. I flit on the edges of fandom, in however that word is defined. And in these tributaries of interest, I might have a discussion. "Have you seen the new Miyazaki movie?"

And I might reply, "I don't like anime."

"All anime?" the person might say with surprise and disgust.

"There are some that are okay, but for the most part, I don't like anime."

"That seems like too broad a stroke."

"Yeah, it probably is."

"You just haven't seen the really good ones. If you watch the good ones, you will change your mind."

"But," I might say, "I'm okay having my mind the way it is."

This is all to say that so much of the media that I took in as a kid in Naperville was Japanese, and a lot of it was anime. Did those programs sour me on all the work I refuse to engage with?

I don't think so. I don't have strong memories of the programs. Speed Racer is more of a cool theme song than a show for me. And Prince Planet is a point of discussion more than TV show. I don't remember ever watching it. I remember that my sister really liked it. I remember discussions with her that it was on at noon. The only way to watch it were the times we came home for from school. School was only two blocks away and we were allowed to walk home for lunch. (Is that for real? Were we allowed, as little kids, to leave school and eat at home while watching Prince Planet? I can't believe that happened? But there are those little memories that tell me that did occur.)

Prince Planet was a member of the Universal Peace Corp. He was on Earth to see if we were worthy of being a member. While he was here, he helped Earth against calamity. He took on an alter-ego of a grade school boy named Bobby. All of this was learned on WikiPedia.

It was in black and white, and so it probably didn't last too long on the TV stations. By the 1970s, there was a shedding of things monochromatic. We wanted vibrant things doing loud acts. We wanted everything to be filled with color.

When I remember this show I cannot recall, I tend to think of it in color. I tend to make every part of it up from whole cloth.

It was my sister's show. She is the one who brings it up. My role in these moments is to agree with her and say that I also thought it was a great show. My job is less witness and more the person brought up to the stand to provide an adequate alibi.

3

Ultra Man

Ultraman is like Superman in America. He is the emblematic character that is bigger than the stories he came from. There are statues and T-Shirts and museums. There is a whole industry built around the character. People who never watch the show know Ultra Man. He is so ubiquitous that people don't even know that he is around. In Japan, you think Ultra Man. We probably see or hear references to Superman all the time. That's what Ultra Man is like. Big as Superman. Faster than a speeding bullet. And Ultraman also gets to turn into a giant. So that's a bonus.

Ultra Man was made in 1966. Science Patrol is the government group that handles monster issues on Earth. That's a big order. Thank goodness that one of their members. Hayata, can turn into Ultraman. And as Ultraman, he has great powers and can even turn into a towering giant. That's a good skill, because every episode, a giant monster comes to do damage to Japan.

Hayata is given a hand-held communication device. He holds it up to the heavens and is transformed into Ultra Man. One time in the show, he accidentally held up a spoon and wondered why he wasn't made different. I guess spoons don't have the kind of magic that the device has.

This is a great early version of giant good-guy versus giant monster genre. I am sure that the Japanese have a frightfully specific language for what this genre is.

But there is no specific language for the people in the show. It is all fake. They obviously were speaking Japanese, but what came out of their mouths was breathless, almost apologetic, rendering of the language.

I feel like I should make a witty comment of two about the strange falseness of the dubbing process, but hasn't that been done all the time? Aren't we bored of that observation. To be fair, a lot of what I watched was dubbed into English. But I don't know when I realized that the actors were not speaking English. I think it came pretty quickly. I don't know if anyone had to tell me, but I think we were all bright enough to notice that something was off with their voices. Those voices did not go with those bodies. Let's not even talk about the fact that the words are divorced from the movement of the mouth.

And the monsters had zippers in their backs. You had to know that something was off with that. And the cities that were destroyed were not real cities. They were toy cities. I had seen enough kidscapes shown in the Sears Catalog to know when something was actual and something was just for play.

It is hard to decide when we, as children, were discerning enough to know that all of this was a hoax, a put upon, make believe and nonsense. Maybe we wanted everything to be nonsense and were willing to embrace it. We didn't want the certainty of school and kids who wouldn't play with us. That was a reality to not embrace.

It was always more appealing, and pleasant, to believe in the giant robots and the monsters that fought them. It was always better to notice the zipper. The zipper was the reassuring pat on the head. The zipper on the back of the monster let us know that there was nothing to be afraid of. The zipper let us know that nothing would tear us down. Because if we pulled on the zipper, we would know what a game it was. What silly fun all this destruction and ferment really is.

4

The Monkees

I had no intention to write about the Monkees. That was never in my plan. The idea of this little book was not to list all the TV shows I stationed myself in front of when I was a boy in Naperville. When I announced I was going to write something about watching shows from that time, my sister was excited. She was surprised about my list of shows I was going to cover. She noticed that it didn't have Super Friends on it. And besides that, where was the Land of the Lost? How could that not be in there? She was shocked that the Monkees was not included.

She mentioned how the two of us and the two Anderson kids would watch the show and act it out. We all had our specific roles. My sister played Mike Nesmith and I was Peter Tork, of all people. I do not remember that. I wonder if I picked it or was the greatness of it thrust upon me.

The Monkees was a fascinating study of falsehood. It was a band only because it was a TV show. They were auditioned to be on a show, not to be a band. The fact that they became one was a fluke of the moment. If they were playing a band and they were singing songs that seemed to be coming from a band, then why shouldn't they be one? No one knows who was the dog and who was the tail in that story.

But I am not interested in going any further. That was the kind of show that played on Channel 9. That was the big time of local Chicago television. Those were the shows that everyone watched and talked about. People would watch Brady Bunch or Gilligan's Island or the Monkees together. Kids would visit other kids's houses to watch the shows as group. Batman was aired on Channel 9. That was a channel that every Television could get.

There were some stations that TVs in basement living rooms were unable to tune. The antenna was pretty stationary. My father, and I am sure all the fathers on the block, would announce to us in the diresest of tones, "Do not play with the antenna. It is perfect and I don't want you messing with it."

Not all broadcast signals came out the same way. Some were strong and persistent. Some were weak and shy. The shy channels were usually UHF. They didn't have the range. They were tough to keep solid and viewable. They were evasive and squiggly.

The TV in our parent's room had two antennas on the top of it and with a little twisting and a little prayer, the small channels could come in. There was Channel 32 that had older TV shows and some weird old movies. But the one that I loved was Channel 44. This was where the forgotten shows lived. This was where the unloved programs found a home. The shows I adored.

As a kid, I spent a lot of time in my parent's room watching those two channels. That's where they lived. The Monkees were too large scale and upmarket for what those stations could afford to view. I didn't know it then. I didn't understand that what I loved was cheap also rans. I didn't know about kitsch and camp. I just knew that these were shows for me and me alone.

5
The Beatles

Most people I talk to are unaware that the Beatles had a cartoon show. Even fans of the band might not know about it.

"I used to watch the Beatles cartoon show every afternoon,"

"What are you talking about? Are you talking about Yellow Submarine? You watched that movie every afternoon?"

"No. I like that movie and it was really well animated, but that's not what I'm talking about. This is an American cartoon show that originally was on Saturday mornings."

"There was a Saturday morning Beatles show? Impossible."

"Well, I don't think it was any good. But it did have three early Beatles songs every episode, so it wasn't that bad when you think of it."

"No. I never heard of it. And if I don't know of it, I am sure you are mistaken. There couldn't have been a show like that."

That's the thing with experts. If they are unaware of something, then that thing cannot be real. But I don't blame that attitude when it comes to the Beatles show. It was pretty bad. The voices were not the Beatles. I had heard them on documentaries and in the movie Help. This was not what they sounded like. The voices were American voice actors pretending to be slightly British. They were probably told not to be sound VERY British, and let's not even talk about giving them a Liverpool twang.

The animation was odd. They looked like squat paper puppets. The stories were goofy. The Beatles traveled a lot and had mad adventures with a wide variety of antagonists. Each seven minute story ended with a lot of chasing about to the sound of a Beatles song. In the middle of the episode there was a sing-a-long where the lyrics were displayed and a bouncing ball let us know what word we should be singing.

As I said, this was great because the Beatles were wonderful to me and this was a way to hear their music. It should go without saying that the days before the digital world meant that, unless we owned all the albums, the only way to hear the songs was at the capricious whim of radio DJs. They might play the song you like, but then again, they probably will not. The cartoon guaranteed that three Beatles songs would be played and all you had to do was survive the limited animation.

We were inundated with box sets from KTel records during the commercials. There was piano classics. There was Zamfir, master of the pan flute. I remember them flouting the greatest hits of Credence Clearwater Revival. Then there was the joy of Dumb Ditties, where we got to listen to very dumb songs made to annoy parents and embolden kids. No matter what they were selling, I always felt they were second rate. The good music was to be found in the records that were never sold during the commercial breaks. The Beatles were too good for such rash salesmanship.

I remember when my mother came home with a two album set of Beatles music. It was the greatest hits album that was red. There was another one that was green, but those were the later more adventurous songs and I was not into that kind of thing. The red album had all the great songs from 1963 to 1965. I took the album as my own and played it all the time. I acted out the stories like Ride My Car or Nowhere Man. I was puzzled by Eleanor Rigby but figured that it was like a horror story and Eleanor and her assistant, Father MacKenzie, were off doing terrible things. I mean, she wears a face that she keeps in the jar by the door. How could I not imagine a Vincent Price type of situation.

The cartoon filled me in on other songs that were not on the album. I loved them all. Sometimes I wanted the stories to speed up so we could get to the songs. When I heard the real Beatles speak, I wondered why they sounded wrong.

6

White Sox Games

The programs I liked on Channel 44 were not always on. They were sometimes preempted by White Sox Games. Chicago has two baseball teams: the Cubs and the White Sox. No one I knew was a White Sox fan. We all followed the Cubs. We marveled at our hero, Dave Kingman. He was a homerun hitter and several times he was in the chase for the most homeruns for the season. He never got that, but watching him was always exciting because there was always a chance for a huge swing that connected. We boys would cheer and jump up and down when he knocked it into the stands.

The White Sox did not have that kind of devotion. They were a lousy team. If they were on Channel 44, I would switch to 32 and see what they might have to entertain me. The rare times I watched the Sox was depressing. It felt like a different game. It was listless. It was also poorly attended. There was no way the camera people could avoid shooting the empty stands. There were a few times I counted how many people were shown in the stands, and it was not a taxing exercise.

I played T-ball like all the other kids in the neighborhood. I was in a T-ball league for two years and when it turned to real pitching, I knew I wanted nothing to do with that. The ball was going to be thrown at me? I never had good eye hand coordination. I knew I was going to get hit. Besides, I was not that great hitting the ball off the T, why would I think that I was going to be better with a pitcher throwing at me.

There was such a sense of nausea when I went up to the T to hit the stationary ball. Everyone was looking at me. My team and the other team and the too too boisterous parents shouting from the bleachers. There was always a chance I was going to just graze the ball, or maybe miss it completely and whiff. The kids laughed when this happened. If I hit it soundly, there was the chance I might get to first base, but I was usually thrown out.

My mother always said I did well. That playing is the fun part, not winning. I just wanted them to not notice me.

I thought of the White Sox games recently. I was flipping channels with my remote control. I didn't have such a luxury as a kid. Not only did I have to adjust the antenna, I had to get up and manually change the channels. I had to make sure the top switch was set to UHF and then I had to move the bottom switch. Such toil. But now I was pressing buttons on the remote control (feeling only slightly winded) and came across a Red Sox game.

This was during the time of Covid and the stands were empty. People might actually want to attend, but they can't. No one was in the stands. I flashed to a moment of deja vu. I remembered seeing things like this. I remembered the 1975 White Sox. I remembered hearing Harry Carey tell people from his announcer's box that it is a great day for baseball and you should come on down to the field and watch a game. Empty like no one likes the team. Empty like the plague.

7

Johnny Sokko and His Flying Robot

Johnny Sokko had the best pet. A robot. A giant robot. With the coolest name ever. Robot. Lest you forget what you're dealing with.

There were no pets in my house. No cats. No dogs. My mother was against animals, wanted nothing to do with furry things. She never liked animals. As a child in Brooklyn, I guess it wasn't a thing. No one had pets on Tahema Street, or at least that was the word we got.

My father liked the idea of suburban life. He was so happy to be in Illinois. He loved being in Naperville. And one of the things people had were dogs. Dogs made the house. He and my sister would pick up stray dogs and sequester them away in the garage. They then would go upstairs and ask my mother if we can have a dog. After the inevitable reply, they released their canine guest, which was no doubt being searched for by its real owner, already plastering the neighborhood with "Have You Seen This Dog" posters.

We were allowed gerbils. The consolation prize of pets. No puppy for you, but look! A desert rat that will look smashing running on a wheel in a repurposed twenty gallon fish tank. To this day, for me, disappointment smells of wood chips.

But a pet robot would alleviate all of that. It doesn't shed, you don't need to feed it. And if any giant monster came to Western Cook County on a rampage of destruction, I would have that covered. How cool would I be? My pet robot stopped VeggaTerrible, the one hundred foot broccoli monster from decimating the Mall. All that Rascal, the Riley's pet dog, could do was kind of roll over and play slightly comatose.

Johnny Sokko was on Channel 44. Johnny was always in shorts. I guess if you have a pet robot, you never have to wear pants. The tale of a boy who becomes accidentally linked with a hundred foot robot, becoming the only one to control it. Every show had a new humongous monster to spar with and defeat. It was bliss.

The final episode was sad, though. I missed most of it when it aired, I was delayed with Cub Scouts. I tuned in to find Johnny Sokko wailing tears for the now absent Robot over gooey string music. He bellowed, "Robot! Robot!"

I am not sure how we got there. To that moment. To those tears. I can only figure that the pet's true owner finally found him and took him back to his rightful home, as these things tend to happen to lonely boys dreaming of a perfect friend.

8

Creature Feature

The weekends were interminable. They stretched out for days. It started good. My sister and I would dispatch ourselves in front of the basement TV and fight over which Saturday Morning cartoon to watch. Some were no brainers, such as Scooby Doo and Super Friends. Then came more existential fights, should we watch Jabber Jaw or Yogi Bear?

By the end of the morning, my sister was off to friends or soccer and I would have the TV to myself, but there was less choice. I would watch Fat Albert out of a sense of completion. It was always the last cartoon showed and if I wanted to watch cartoons, then this was it.

Then what was I to do for the rest of the day? Ride my bike and see if someone wanted to play? I would go to the park by myself if no one wanted to play. It was a safe neighborhood, meaning that no one seemed to mind if some kid was in your yard. I am sure the doors were rarely locked.

Sundays were worse. There were no good cartoons, and everyone was away with church or family or both. We were the Jewish family in the neighborhood. There were Jews in Naperville, but not a hell of a lot. I was asked more than once, "Why don't you go to church."

"We're Jewish, we don't go to church. We could go to temple on Saturday, but we usually don't." This never seemed to placate these kids. They seemed resentful. Was I beaten up by a few of these inquisitors? A few times, but I am sure that it had nothing to do with me being Jewish. Positive. This was the time of Skokie, Illinois and the struggle of the American Nazi party to march in a Jewish area. Yeah, there were no issue there.

If I could get away with it, I would slink back into the house and watch more TV. My father would see me and tell me to play outside. "I did. Now I'm done." It wasn't really worth the fight, and I was mostly allowed my sloth.

Both 32 and 44 had horror movies on Saturday and Sunday afternoons. They might have had a name for the block, but I can't remember. In my mind I have assigned the name Creature Feature, though I am pretty sure that wasn't it. How to Make a Monster. I Was a Teen Age Werewolf. The Fall of the House of Usher. Drive-in fodder that was cheap for the stations to air.

They were all old and cheesy. I was still petrified by them. My mother recalls that I would watch these monstrosities under a blanket, only peaking out at an angle, looking from the edge. My mother would tell me that I didn't need to watch these things if they scared me.

According to my mother, my reply was always, "I'm watching these so I won't be scared anymore." These are brave words and I am sure they were complete bullshit. I was scared and scared I remained.

Channel 32 had pretty good movies. They were scary and decent. Sometimes they even did a Godzilla movie, which wasn't scary, but they were Godzilla and that's always good. A giant rampaging lizard is always a delight.

Channel 44 had weird movies. They didn't have the good ones. I knew this. I sensed it. But they were still pretty cool. The best were the Sampson movies. They were Mexican wrestling movies that starred Sampson. These were the American versions, because the wrestler was actually called Santos. But I knew him as Sampson. He was in his forties, going to paunch, and always wearing a silver mask.

He would be up against the Aztec Mummy or the Vampire Queen. There would be a lot of driving of cars and then a good deal of wrestling. Usually, the big fight wound up in the ring. Aztec mummies don't wrestle as well as middle-aged luchadors.

Sampson (Santos) never took off his mask. The movies were black and white and somehow the lack of color made this odd fact more palatable. Of course, in a black and white world people would never take their masks off. He would be eating in a swank Mexico City restaurant and then get into his sports car. He wore turtlenecks and blazers, and I am sure they matched his mask. I didn't see this as a trope from a different culture. I saw this as something that everyone did back in the ancient 1960, when no one lived in color.

These movies were not scary. They were cool. I would jump around my parents's room, mimicking the wrestling moves. Sometimes I knocked over pictures. A few knick knacks got broken. I would try to fix things up as well as I could and hope that my mother would find out about it before my dad. My father was a sweet man, but his temper surprised me at times. Those times, when he lost it with me, those were the truly scary moments. The times I would want to hide under a blanket and peer out from the edges.

9

Spider-Man

Spider-Man had a theme song almost as rocking as the Speed Racer theme. The Ramones did a cover of the Spider-Man song, and that is some twisted street cred for a low budget cartoon show.

The show was full of color and crazed characters. I loved it. I never read Spider-Man comics, but I was sure it was just like this.

What I loved about it was that it was kind of boring. I didn't know this at the time, but for the third season, they cut the budget to make each episode. So the director, Ralph Bakshi, put in a lot of filler.

There were whole minutes of Spider-Man swinging from building to building on his way to the big emergency. He swung to the left. He swung to the right. He swung straight ahead. Sometimes, he planted himself on the side of the building and paused in a moment of quiet reflection.

These scenes were the exact ones from the episode before. It was filler. And I loved it because it was dull. Who needed all that excitement. Sometimes the fun part is the journey. Even if the journey was the same one that is shown all the time. Repetition is not bad. Boredom is not bad. Even superheroes have to do the drudge work.

I didn't like school. But the walk was nice. It was brief and there was always something to see. The houses looked all the same and that fascinated me. Spider-Man swung from building to building. It was kind of a drag, but it must have felt nice to be out in the air, moving forward.

10

Ray Rayner and Friends

This was a Channel Nine show. This was the big time for kids shows. It doesn't fit into this survey of my bargain basement television youth, but it was part of my viewing. It was an important part of the day. The show was originally called Breakfast with Bugs Bunny. And isn't breakfast the most important meal of the day? Even if what you are feasting on is old cartoons? It is a necessary thing to consume.

Ray Rayner was an old guy who did a show for kids. He wasn't old in the perspective of a five year old. He was old even for television. He was in his mid fifties. His show went on for nearly twenty years. He retired from it at the age of 60.

He was a guy with a mop of tan hair who always wore a colorful jumpsuit. The jumpsuit was to show that he was fun. I remember him always wearing an orange jumpsuit, but pictures I have accessed show different colors.

He was unassuming. He wasn't loud or flashy. He was on at seven in the morning, before the coffee kicked in.

He told what the weather was. He went through the news of the day. He announced the sports scores. I have a vague memory of him also stating school cancelations due to snow, but was there any snow days in Illinois? Didn't we go to school no matter what? That's my memory. But how good is that?

He said this and said that, and it felt like a news reader. Then, all of a sudden, with no warning, he would say, "Cartoon." And like that, an old Looney Tunes cartoon would start. There were four or five cartoons on any of his shows. I loved Bugs Bunny.

I don't know if I liked Ray Rayner or if I just tolerated him. He was the old guy I had to hang with to get my cartoons. He was nice. I think there were some skits with a puppet dog. He would announce birthdays for the kids in the audience.

I know one of the big events of the year for Ray Rayner was the Christmas Time Jelly Bean Contest. He would display a small plastic house filled with jelly beans and we were allowed to send in a postcard to guess how many jelly beans there were. This was exciting. No, I guess it wasn't, but every year I really wanted to get the right number. I think I sent in my guess a few years. The winner would get to be on the show and get prizes like a year's supply of soda or something like that.

There was nothing wrong with Ray Rayner, but as an adult I have always been puzzled by the tradition of having cartoon shows be hosted by grown-ups in odd costumes. Every television market had an aging actor who cavorted before the camera and talked to puppets and introduced antiquated cartoons. Why did we need the grown-ups? Did they validate our love of Daffy Duck? If you watch some of the clips of the old shows on YouTube, you might find them kind of creepy. But that's me, an adult talking.

About ten years ago, my friend Ken, who manages a large comic book store in Worcester, told me he was excited because he booked Rex Trailer to an in-store appearance. He was kind of scared because he had to lay out some money to get him and he wasn't sure if he would break even. He didn't know if anyone would even remember Rex Trailer.

I didn't remember him. I had no clue. Ken looked dejected when I told him that I didn't know who he was. He explained that for 20 years, Rex had a children's show out of Boston called Boomtown. There were Wild West shenanigans. It was really popular. He sang songs like Pow Wow the Pony. I didn't know what to say. I know that if I had a chance to meet Ray Rayner all these years later, I probably would pass. I don't know what I might say to him.

My wife convinced me to go to the event. "Look, if no one shows, at least you will be there." She was right. I went. And the place was jammed. There were people in every aisle. There was a long line of middle aged men and women waiting patiently to meet the eighty year old Rex Trailer and get something signed. They all seemed excited to be there. Every few minutes, Rex would stop the signing and play one of his cowboy songs on his guitar. Then he would happily sit down and meet another former child who was excited to be there. To see him in person at long last.

Ken was smiling to beat the band. I still don't know how I feel about the grown-ups doling out the cartoons to the kids, but for some, they were happy to have a friend spend the early morning hours with them.

11

The Invisible Man

No one could see him. No one knew who he was. His identity was as solid as the light that passed right through him. The Invisible Man.

It played on Channel 44 on the weekends. That was the time to play adventure oriented shows. All of them were old. All of them were in Black and White.

In this version of the story, the Invisible Man was a kind hearted scientist who helps the British government. Why wouldn't they want a spy no one could see?

I liked the idea of not being seen. Oh, the fun I could have if no one could find me. Actually, I spent many hours watching television upstairs or riding my bike around the neighborhood. No one seemed to be looking for me. Maybe I was invisible. Maybe I was unseen all this time.

I noticed something about the show, they never said who played the Invisible Man.The credits said that the Invisible Man was played by himself. I knew this was not true. I knew that invisible men in tv shows were all done with wires and sleight of hand. I knew the Invisible Man was not real. He couldn't be. He wouldn't allow himself to be the lead of a show if he was real.

But why would they not say what actor did the voice? Why were not allowed to know? What secret could there be?

Maybe it was someone we knew. Maybe it was a friend of a family. Maybe it was the Uncle we never saw. Maybe it was me. Maybe I was just too proud or too shy to take the proper credit.

12

The Channel 44 Christmas Special

Like Ray Raynor and Friends, Channel 44 had a cartoon show that featured live hosts. But that is where the comparison ended. There were two hosts, a man and a woman. They were also not middle aged or dressed in anything silly. They were young and dressed like real people who you might see outside of a TV screen. I liked them. I don't remember what their schtick was, but they were personable. Knowing the kind of material Channel 44 had to offer, I am sure they had the lamest cartoons.

They were like grown-ups who could talk about comic books and other important things. Sometime around December they began promoting their special Christmas day episode where they would be playing Christmas classics and lots of special treats. I was excited about this. I wondered what they would be showing for us. I made sure that after Santa delivered all the presents (we were Jewish but my father wasn't and so somehow we had Santa) I went up to my parents's room and turned on the television, There was an old movie playing. I think it was boring. I think I changed the channel to other things and looked back to see if anything exciting might occur.

I was lucky and found my two friends, the two hosts meeting each other. The set was adorned in Holiday cheer. They were dressed casually. It seemed like they were just arriving. They wished each other a Merry Christmas and then hugged and kissed. On the lips.

What the?

The two hosts kissed? They acted like gross grown-ups. They were just giving each other a holiday greeting, but who does that for a greeting? It bothered me. It made me think that some rule had been violated. This was not cool.

They were young. This was the 70s. I suppose this was a typical type of hello for their group and they were letting their hair down for this special episode. And it was wrong. Don't act like grown-ups. Act like kids. Like your cartoons. Like your audience.

My sense of betrayal has stayed with me all these years. I couldn't believe they did that and when I recall it, I am still annoyed. I am sure that this was not a great job for them. This was the cheapest station in Chicago. They probably had other jobs in the station just to get a paycheck. The show might be something they did for free. Was it a perk for working at the station that was forced to play White Sox games?

That show was not on for much longer. I am sure it was too expensive to make compared to playing reruns of old Japanese TV shows. It wasn't cost effective. Few of these things were.

13

Bozo's Circus

Bozo's Circus was on Channel Nine everyday at noon. It was the big kids's show. Men in clown suits cavorted around while a studio audience of kids watched. Kids got to play games, like throw balls in buckets, or something like that.

I loved this show. I wanted to be on it. My mother always said, "We'll see. We'll see." Which even I knew meant, not a chance in hell. I only got to see it when I was sick or I went home for lunch.

My biggest memory of the show was one not of the main characters of Bozo, Cookie and the Ring Leader announcer, but of Jim Dale. I think it was Jim Dale. The movie Pete's Dragon was coming out and Jim Dale was going around publicizing it. He played the evil snake oil salesman. He and Red Buttons had a number were they sang about all the amazing properties dragon parts have. It's a funny song.

My memory is that Jim Dale and maybe Red Buttons came on the Bozo show, dressed up as their characters. They talked about the movie and then they sang the song. I felt like it was a special show just for me. I still feel an affinity for Jim Dale all these years later (like when my son and I listened to him read the Harry Potter books on CD) and that we are old pals he and I. He survived the Bozo show, and I witnessed it for him.

In preparation to writing this, I found an episode of the Bozo show on YouTube. It was from much later than my day. It was from 1992. I am amazed that it was still on at that late date. The set looked smaller, dingier. Maybe the years wore it down, maybe it was always like that. The Bozo from that episode had four kids ready to play a game, He introduced them all by saying this one was handsome and this one was pretty. He put his hands on their shoulders as he spoke to them. It was so creepy to me. I thought I saw the look of panic in one of the contestant's eyes. This would not be a treasured memory of youth for her. This was the beginning of the fear of clowns and a general distrust of grown-ups.

Suddenly, I knew why my mother never worked too hard about getting us to Chicago to see the show.

14

Captain Fathom

No place but Channel 44 would play this. They probably bought it for five bucks a show, and even that might have been too pricey.

This was a show from the early 60s that came out by Cambria Studios. It was directed by the amazing comic book artist, Alex Toth.

I watched it every now and then but I never followed the plot. I never knew what was going on. I was too busy paying attention to the mouths. The mouths were not right.

The pictures were mostly stationary. They hardly had any true animation. But the mouths of the characters when they talked would come to life and move in human ways. And the mouths looked just like normal mouths with teeth and tongue. What the hell was this? I was fascinated and repulsed.

Cambria used a process called syncro-vox to save money. They didn't have to synch the voice to an animated mouth. Instead, they filmed someone speaking the dialogue and then superimposed the image of the mouth over a stationary drawing of the character. It saved money. And it was so disturbing.

This was my version of rubbernecking. I watched Captain Fathom in small bites. I focused on the teeth that were shown. Perhaps the story was good. Maybe amazing fits of adventure occurred. All I saw were the human mouths floating about drawings pretending to be something alive.

15

Marvel Superheroes

I am astounded by how much television I watched. This little survey will not even get close to discussing all the shows I watched and studied and learned by heart. There were times I would watch lousy reruns of Love American Style because someone else in the house insisted it be on. Or Petticoat Junction or Green Acres or all the other shows I watched because it was television.

But I did things as well. Where was the time found? I was in cub scouts. I played with the kids across the street. I had friends I could visit if I rode my bike a few blocks away. I was allowed to walk to the drug store and buy comics. I loved comics. I spent a lot of time reading and re-reading them. I listened to records and acted out what I heard. I made great plays that I would perform in my room. I was in soccer. I was in a kid's bowling league. I was tortured by my family when we all went ice skating, a skill I never had. There were movies and outings and plays in Chicago. My mother hated living in the suburbs and always insisted on museums and art. She was preparing us for the time we might escape back to New York, I suppose.

The question remains, how was there so much time in the life of a kid? I am not quite sure. It is one of those mysteries. TIme is short. And the days were all so long.

I did multi-task in one way. There was a show on Channel 44 that took up some of my comic book reading. It was a wonderful show called the Marvel Superheroes. There were serialized stories of: Captain America, Iron Man, Thor, Submariner and the Hulk. It was done by the same company that did the Spider-Man show, so the animation was bad and the theme songs were rocking. The one for the Hulk still makes me smile.

These were made in the mid sixties and they were exciting. The reason they were is that they were taken directly from the Marvel Comics of the day. They took the illustrations from the comics and applied basic limited animation to them. So what we watched was the actual art of Jack Kirby come slightly to life. The stories took the Stan Lee dialogue and changed hardly anything. If you wanted to read hard to find Marvel comics, this was a great way. I felt like I was expanding my superhero acumen by watching them. And the theme songs. The theme songs were awesome.

It was only years later that I found out the dark side to this show. The original comic artists who first drew them: Jack Kirby, Don Heck, Steve Ditko, Mary Severin; got nothing. They received no additional pay for their art being broadcast. They created these iconic characters and received nothing for it.

When I watched it as a kid, I knew nothing about this. I was innocent. I was complicit. I was having a good time singing along, "When Captain America throws his mighty shield."

16

Space Giants

This was on Channel 44 and it was my favorite show. Just the name alone brought me pleasure. I loved it. None of my friends at school had ever heard of it. It was just two words crashed together. That was one of the joys of that show, no one knew it. It was mine and mine alone. I don't think anyone else watched Channel 44. It was my private station for my personal entertainment, like I was a seven year old Cesar with all the breads circuses..

I might mention the name Space Giants to another kid and hold my breath waiting for his reply. "Is that really a show, or did you make it up?" I would swear that it was real. They could watch it if they wanted it. It was on every afternoon/ "Why would I want to watch that, it sounds stupid."

Maybe I did make it up. Maybe it was a figment of my imagination. When I got older, and hung out with other science fiction lovers, I might float the name out to them and they didn't know it. It was a mystery. Johnny Sokko and Ultra Man were Japanese giant monster shows that people knew. But Space Giants.

And they didn't know what they were missing.

It was the best.

It was originally called Ambassador Magma when it was in Japan, but now with the English coming from their mouths, it was Space Giants and the main character was a giant gold robot called Goldar. He had wife named Silvar. They had a child who had antenna on his head and could turn into a rocket plane. They were fighting the evil monster-rabble-rouser Rodak who brought forth dinosaur monsters. Every episode ended with a fight between Goldar and the monster of the week.

I wish I could tell you why this show was so great. It just was. It was better than Ultra Man and the rest. It made me happy.

The other day, I watched an episode of it on YouTube. I have no idea what I liked about it. It really was silly and didn't have the charm I recall it possessing. Did I change? Did it? I have to say I am slightly disappointed. I am happy that I loved it so much back then. I just don't see it now. But why do we expect ourselves to love the same things we did when we were kids? Are we not allowed to change, to alter?

Shows did not last long on Channel 44. They were always looking for the next cheap ass show that will be a ratings sensation. Space Giants left and was replaced by another giant monster show from Japan. I cannot recall what it was, just that it wasn't good. It was silly and it just was no Space Giants. I watched it for a spell because of my affection for Space Giants, but the lack of that charm made me look for other things to watch, or maybe I even went outside to see what magic was there.

I was once told that if the commercial breaks are filled with promos for other shows or public service announcements, then that was a show they couldn't sell the ad space for and the show was generating no revenue.

I seem to recall a lot of public service announcements and ads for other shows and movies when I watched Channel 44. I was watching shows for free. No one considered me enough of a market to even try to sell to me.

This made the shows purer. Space Giants were not pimping themselves for the latest cereal or the K Tell record box set. No. Space Giants were there for that one kid savvy enough to know how great it was. Saving the world day after day, at no extra charge.

17

The Peoria Pig Report

When I told people that this was the latest little memoir I was writing, my sister started listing all the shows we watched and loved. The list, that included Kimba the White Lion, were her shows. I might have watched them, but there was a clear line that was drawn. I had my shows, and she had hers. We might be able to like the same ones, but one of us owned that show, and don't you forget it.

She then wrote that, "We used to watch the Peoria Pig Report before Super Friends came on."

What?

We watched what?

I asked her to further explain, but she never got back to me. Maybe she expected me to remember it on my own. I do not.

I do not know or have an inkling. Some research informed me that Peoria, until recently, was a major hub for hog sales. It stands to reason, that in those more rural days, there would be a television news show about the hog trade.

I looked for any evidence of the show on the internet and was unsuccessful. Why would no one put this show on YouTube?

And now I am left with a void. I suddenly want nothing more than to watch vintage episodes of the Peoria Pig Report. I would have favorite scenes. I would proudly wear the t-shirt.

And to think, this was a ritual. One cannot properly enjoy the Super Friends without learning about the sale of pigs in nearby Peoria. There was an order to how we watched things. But what is the use of such order if you can't remember it?

That's the thing with memory. It's a lot like tuning a weak signal into the television set by twisting the antenna this way and that. Sometimes you are blessed with a strong signal and the memory is there all crisp and vibrant. Other times, no matter what you do with the antenna, it comes in grainy and unclear. Then there are the times that you just can't get the channel at all. You might get a stray bit of dialogue, but for the most part, you are seeing nothing but static and uncertainty.

It's a joy to remember the things that meant something to you when you were a kid. But how many of those memories were sent out by a small transmitter? One that was not expected to get to the next town, or to the next forty years? We are lucky we can pick up any signal at all. It's amazing we still have a history to share.

18

Marlo and the Magic Movie Machine

Marlo and the Magic Movie Machine was one of those misfit kid shows that were not made for Saturday morning. This was one for Sunday morning, so it had a little bit more of an educational bent. It was on the CBS affiliate. Imagine that, we have made it to the big time stations at last.

My sister and I always watched it together. I don't know why. Maybe because it was the only thing on, and it wasn't too bad, so why not?

The premise was that Marlo worked at a large computer company in the basement. When it was quitting time, instead of going home, he would go into a secret room, put on some goofy clothes and turn on the Machine.

The Machine was a pleasant, giant computer. They would read letters from viewers. They would tell jokes. Marlo always had a whiny sort of way he talked to his buddy, "Machine."

I think the premise was that Machine would send Marlo off to discover different cultures or locations. There would be film of him learning about these things and then he would come back. I am not sure, I watched one episode recently and that seems to be what the premise was.

Then he would return and he would sadly say, "Goodnight, Machine."

My sister and I were watching this, playing around and making jokes, when my mother called us up to her room. We were having a grand time, blowing off steam while watching Marlo. I think I was still smiling when I entered the bedroom.

This is the way I remember it. Other people have different memories of that morning. I am the only who thinks it was on Sunday. I am the only who brings up Marlo and the Magic Movie Machine.

My mother was in bed. Next to her was my grandmother. She had arrived a few days ago, after my father was taken to the hospital. He had a heart attack due to his diabetes. I had not seen him in days. My mother did not take me to see him.

Of course. This was the moment my mother told us that he was dead. He never really survived the heart attack.

I don't know much about the conversation or the days after that. Everything was surrounded by static.

I never forgave myself for laughing when I came into the bedroom to get the news. I never forgave myself for enjoying myself. I never forgave Marlo or the Machine, either. There was plenty of blame to spread around.

19

Star Blazers

I watched Star Blazers in 1979. That whole year was taken up with my mother's plan to move back to New York. We only moved to Illinois because my father's job transferred all of us there. She never liked it. The huge blizzard that winter was the final straw. When she had to hire a local high school kid to shovel the snow off the roof of the house for fear of structural issues, she knew she could not stand another year there.

My sister was devastated by the news. I was not too excited either, but I was alright. I always had friends, but I didn't feel like any of the ties were permanent.

Star Blazers was a complex science fiction animated show from Japan. The Earth was attacked by the Gamilon, alien humanoids with blue skins. The Gamilons radiated the Earth and all life was to die soon. Earth was given hope from a distant planet. They had a device to clean the Earth's atmosphere of the radiation, but the people of Earth had to travel across space to get it. A group fitted up an old World War 2 warship as a spaceship and traveled to the destination across the stars, all while being attacked by the Gamilon.

Every episode was more and more tense. Each half hour ended with the narrator saying how many days were left before the Earth was destroyed. The numbers ticked down every day. There was not enough time left for anyone to make it.

I ran home to watch this. This was on one of the bigger stations. This was a big deal. Other kids even talked about watching it. Star Blazers was not one of those shows that seemed to have an audience of one.

It was getting closer to the big deadline, where we would find out if the Star Blazers, in their warship space vehicle, The Yamamoto, would get the device in time and save everyone. But the deadline for me was up too. We were moving at the end of October. That was around the time the story for Star Blazers was going to wrap up.

We drove to New York. We got to the town outside of New York City and moved into the condo that was now our home. We unpacked. We wandered around the town that now claimed us as residents. I started school. I tried to get along. I tried to make friends. I found a nearby convenience store that sold comic books. I did things to feel normal.

It was several weeks before I found the TV station that was playing Star Blazers. When I finally got to see it, I was confused. The bad guys were not blue skinned anymore. They were green skinned. Could the animators just have made a mistake and painted the wrong color on them?

No. These were new bad guys. New things were happening. Many of the main cast were dead or gone since I last checked in on them. They had a new crisis to avert. They had new issues. They had not waited for me.

I watched the whole episode sitting two feet from the large TV in the mostly unpacked living room of our new place.

That was the last time I watched the show.

Completed November 17. 2020 at 7AM

The Criteria for Calm

This was begun at 8:45 on Tuesday the 19th of January, 2021

1

A Proposition

While we were both restraining an aggressive student on the ground, she asked me on a date. It was seven in the morning and the student had just gotten out of the shower. He was naked except for a pair of BVDs and he was soapy and keeping a grip on his arm was tough. I was on the left arm. I had the student's arm in one hand while my other hand was pressing his shoulder down. Another staff had the other arm and a third had bite guard. The girl, the one who was about to ask me on a date, was on legs. She was lying across both legs, her arm was wrapped around them. The student had himself some early morning strength and was moving his legs ups and down. The girl was riding the legs.

Eventually, it settled. The lead teacher stated that he had calm on his side, but me and the other two said we didn't. That meant we kept on going. A fifth staff, watching, checked her watch and said, "Ten minutes."

Things were quieting down, but the student was still moving and fighting. That was not calm and we kept on until we had it. I looked behind me, to check on the girl. The legs had gotten quiet and she was just lying there now. "Hey," she said.

"Hey," I said back.

"So, how are you liking the job," she asked.

I was a month into the teaching position. "It's great." That's what we quickly learned to say. The job wasn't tough. The job wasn't awful. It certainly was not just okay. Everything had to be great. We only survived on our hyperbole.

The lead teacher, the one on the right side, shouted, "Focus."

We went for another minute. One of us said, "Calm." That was followed by another saying, "Not calm." We all needed thirty seconds of calm body before we released.

"Hey," the girl said,

"Hey," I said back.

"What are you doing tonight?"

"Nothing," I said. My shift was over at three. Then I would drive my awful car back to my awful apartment and will myself to not be bruised.

She flashed a smile. "You want to go for a drink. Not across the street. I know a place. They have food, too. What do you say."

"Focus," the lead teacher said again.

"Sure," I replied. I wasn't sure who I was responding to: the girl or the lead teacher.

"Great," the girl said. "Let's do it for seven."

"Calm," the lead teacher said.

"Calm," I said.

"Calm," the girl said.

That was a quorum. We broke in stages. First the girl moved off the legs. Then I moved off. Then the lead teacher and the guy who had bite guard. The student sat up quickly. He slashed his arm in front of his chest. It didn't hit anyone. It was just a way to say that this wasn't over. Not by any chance. None of this was over. There was no calm here. We were just in a brief moment of grace..

The lead teacher went to the table to get the restraint form. He had some writing to do. The guy who had bite guard redirected the student back to his bedroom where he would finish getting dressed. The girl bounded over to me and pressed her chest into me. She pushed a folded piece of paper into my palm and went back to the students she was assigned to.

The paper had "7pm" on it as well as a phone number. She also had written her name, as if I had many female teachers asking me for a date while restraining a kid and I needed to keep all of them straight in my head.

2

A Definition

Like any job, there are terms and pieces of jargon. For the act of holding another person down until they accede control to another, there are a lot of terms. Prone. Seated. Supine. They all had their specific meanings. Even when we used the word, calm, we were perpetrating jargon. Because we weren't looking for calm when we said it. We were looking for surrender. We were expecting the fire to be extinguished. Calm meant that they did not fight us holding them down for thirty seconds. Calm meant we could let them go, for now. It didn't mean calm like you and I mean it. There is no calm in the student who is just released from a hold. There is only a pause before the next round is rung in.

The term that might take a little explanation is bite guard. I don't know how prevalent that piece of a jargon was. We used it all the time. Bite guard was something one of the teachers did to the student. If the student was known to be a biter or was trying to bite one of the teachers holding him down by the shoulder, then someone would shout, "Bite." And a teacher not otherwise engaged would jump in to give a bite guard.

The process took a little finesse. The thumb opened away from the rest of the fingers. The teacher then put their hand underneath the student's jaw. Some pressure was applied. This didn't shut the mouth, but it controlled the range of motion. If you had a good bite guard, then the teachers probably would not be bit. At least at that moment.

There were many times when we would hear that teacher say, "Got bite." And then after the student moved and thrashed, we might hear the dreaded, "Lost bite." At that point, we were thinking, "Get going, you son of a bitch. Get the bite."

Bites were the worst. Some people really hated hair pulls, and they did suck. But it was bites. Bites that seared your body with abject pain.

You wore the bruises of bites the longest. Bite wounds always had the most colorful bruises. They made modern art on your flesh.

We were obsessed with bites and bite guard. A person who did a good bite guard was everyone's friend.

3

Welcome to the New Job

It was only after a week on the job that I did my first anal probe. We had a student in our residence who would find anything pointy, like nails or screws or pen caps and use them as weapons. He was smart enough to wait until we were unaware and then stab at us. To keep his precious weapons secret, he shoved them up his rectum until he needed them. Because of this, we had to do body searches twice a day.

He had to go into the time-out room, strip and we would then look at his whole body. He had to open up his mouth and show us there was nothing under his tongue. Then he had to bend over and one of us, with a latex glove on, had to check his rectum.

On my first Saturday shift, it was my turn. All the teachers had to do one weekend day on their schedule. Those days were twelve hours long. We went from eight in the morning to eight at night. On my first 12 hour Saturday, I got rectum duty.

It was horrible.

But with this student, he didn't need weapons to make his presence felt. On that weekend, we had carryover from veteran staff helping to train us new teachers. One of the veterans was leaving the school and leaving the field of education. After one year, she had had enough. She was good at showing us what we needed to do. This was her last day working here. After that, she wasn't sure what she was going to do. She knew it wasn't going to be something like this.

In the afternoon, the student said a violent statement, which in his plan had us prompt him to the time out room. The veteran teacher walked next to him as he entered the room. The student stopped and threw his hand backwards. His fist collided with the veteran teacher's ear. She fell down in pain.

Three of us rushed the student and pushed him into the time out room and closed the door. The door could be closed as long as the person closing it kept an eye on the student through an eyepiece.

The veteran teacher tried to shake it off, but was still in major pain. A supervisor was called and he took her to the ER. By the end of our shift, we found out that the veteran teacher had a ruptured eardrum. On her last day.

I was eight days into my time at the school and I discovered that this is how people left the job. With broken bodies and throbbing pain.

4

The School

What is this place?

It was a highly respected special needs school that also had a residential component. Throughout the area, the school had purchased houses and converted them into residences for up to 8 kids. The kids mostly had autism diagnosis. Some of them were outliers. But most were severely challenged.

There was very little in the way of decorations. There were wooden tables and wooden chairs. There were big blocky sofas with wooden frames. There were two to three beds in each room. At night, two staff stayed up, making sure the students slept and didn't cause much mischief.

During the weekdays, the day staff would arrive at 7 and get the kids fed and dressed and then loaded into large passenger vans.

They then went to the school where they learned through discrete trial training. They were always with the same eight kids. There was little intermingling. Each residence was called a team.

My residence was a tough group. Some of the students were verbal, while half were not. There was a good deal of aggression. We were not a staff intensive team. We didn't have seven or eight staff on at any time. We usually had four staff on working with the eight kids, with one or two staff doing administrative duties. We did have two very aggressive students. One was staffed at two to one. There needed to be two staff with this one student. She was a slight young woman of sixteen. She was five foot two and weighed a hundred and twenty pounds and she could break you in half if you gave her a moment to try it.

We worked in the school. We worked in the residence. We worked in the in-between times, when we transported them in the van.

Our students were mostly older teens. We were only a few years older than them. We were their contemporaries. We made around 19 thousand a year. Even then, in the mid 1990s, that was pretty shitty. We lived in cheap apartments with other teachers at the school. We ate the food provided for the students. We drank bad beer because it was the type we could afford. When we went out on our days off, we tended to go out with other teachers from the school. We usually were loud and obnoxious.

We were teachers, because that's what they called us. We ran programs and followed behavior plans. We held kids down when they met criteria. We did what we were told. And we were so damned young.

5

Back-Up

After about twenty seconds, I realized that I was not able to breathe and this is what suffocation felt like. I was getting weak and there was no more fight in me. The student had me in a tight headlock and his whole body was on top of me on the couch.

I sort of remembered how we got in this position. I was with another student in the dining room area. A teacher shouted, "Staff," and I went running. That was what we did. We heard the word "Staff" and we knew that someone needed help. The teacher who shouted it was with a tough student. She was kind of afraid of the student. You couldn't blame her. Though I kind of did.

As soon as I came and put my hand on the student to assist in escorting him to the time out room, I realized I was alone with the student. The other teacher had ran to the kitchen. I had hands on him, I stupidly thought I would be able to get the kid the ten paces to the time out room by myself. I was half way there when the student moved his weight on me and I tumbled over the back end of the sturdy couch. The kid was on me in a second. He was choking me out.

At the edge of my vision, there were pops of color and void. I was excited because now I finally understood what it meant when people said that they had seen stars before their eyes. It wasn't stars or anything celestial, though. What we had here was lack of vision due to an absence of oxygen. But I thought that you could make a fine case for saying that you were seeing stars.

My life did not flash before my eyes. I didn't have the concentration for that.

And I wasn't afraid at all.

Because I heard the heavy footsteps of another staff bounding down the stairs to help me. I didn't know what staff was coming, but that I was going to be okay. Staff was called. Staff came.

I didn't know this at the time, but it was my friend Chris who barreled toward me. He quickly saw what was happening and decided to not follow protocol. He leaped over the couch and clotheslined the student. The kid broke his grip and I reacquainted myself with air.

My eyes focused and I saw my friend holding the kid on the floor. I jumped to and took the other arm. A third staff showed and we got him stabilized and was eventually able to transport him to the time out room.

Filling out the restraint form was a little bit like writing fiction. "I was able to gently put pressure on the student's shoulder and elbow, allowing the teacher being choked to be free and then we followed take down procedures and follow a three person prone restraint."

It might not have been factual. But it read good. It breathed and seemed possible.

6

The Well Dressed Teacher

We wore jean jackets. This stopped some of the scratching. Most of us wore baseball caps. This was to decrease hair pulling. I wore my cap backwards. I must have looked very hip.

Depending on which team you were on, you wore other pieces of sartorial expediency. We put on hockey arm guards. They slid over our hands and encased our upper arms. This was a good way to deal with bites.

We also had a student who was amazing at scratching when we had her in a hold. She was able to move her fingers and bloody us up. For that reason, we also donned batting gloves. They protected our fingers and were supposed to be thin enough so that we could still write down data and reports. This was never easy for me.

When I wrote anything, I had to shed the jeans jacket, take off the arm guards, remove the gloves and then write. Then I had to wrestle the gloves, the arm guards and the jean jacket back on. Eventually, I stopped wearing the gloves. It was just easier to get cut up and bloody then to go through that all the time.

We were an army of young people dressed in our armor. Looking the same as everyone else. We were all so plain and beautiful.

7

The Speed of Things

Let me just say, I did this. This is what happened. I was in the kitchen with a few students and another staff. We were cleaning up after dinner. From the second floor of the residence came a loud, "Staff." I looked at the other staff and she nodded to me. Given permission, I bolted across the entire first floor to the stairs. I flew up the stairs, hardly even touching them.

When I reached the second floor, I was faced with the dilemma of where the incident was occurring. There have been times when I would race around looking for the problem and not being able to locate one. This time, I took a chance and headed to the large boys room.

I ran to the entrance and saw that a student was naked and wet on the floor after coming from the shower. He was encircled by three staff, though they did not have him secure yet.

I continued running towards them and I skidded on a puddle in the middle of the floor. I fell to my hands and knees, but my forward momentum pushed me forward toward the bodies. I skidded into the body of the student and immediately reached for the loose arm. I secured it and got into position for the restraint. From the staff call to me crashing in, fifteen seconds elapsed. One of the teachers couldn't stop laughing at me and my skidding into position.

The procedure took ten minutes and when I told them I ran from the kitchen, no one believed me. I must have been upstairs already but didn't want to admit it because I was not where I was scheduled to be. But no, I did run and I did get there. They nodded their heads. Yeah, sure. Whatever you say, buddy.

8

All This and a Show

If you had to be in a restraint, I preferred it at the residence than at the school. At the residence, it was just the staff you always worked with and trusted (or at least tried to trust). If you are at the school, there is a chance that there will be an audience. There might be other staff watching us, judging us no doubt.

If the restraint happened in a hallway, we would always have rubbernecking gawkers. They would cross their arms and ask if we needed help. That was what we were supposed to do. We were not to jump in on another team's restraint. We were to ask if they needed help. And when asked, the team invariably would say no.

No team wanted to look weak. They didn't want any judging eyes on them, wondering why they couldn't handle something as simple as a four person prone restraint with bite guard in a cramped hallway. I mean, that stuff is easy.

And the thing was, they wouldn't leave. They just stood there, watching us struggle and flop. They must have had something better to do, but still they stood and watched.

The worst, to me at any rate, were the teachers from the staff intensive teams. They always lingered, watching us. Sometimes there were two of them, as they traveled in packs, and whispered back and forth to each other, like they were watching rival chess players. Oh. They were so smug with their five to six restraints a day.

It had the look of verdict on their small grins. One of them watched us dealing with a difficult restraint and came over, "I can help you guys out." We said no. The truth was, he really could help us out, but why admit that? Why should we run a restraint procedure better and more efficiently instead of protecting our sense of pride?

And besides, that guy was probably an asshole.

I didn't want to be watched. I was never the best at restraints. Being good at them meant that everyone was safe and protected. I wasn't bad at them. I did what was expected. But I never was put on the Restraint All Star team. I don't think there ever was a team like that, but if there was, I wasn't on it.

9
Killing Time

The twelve-hour weekend shifts were interminable. They just went on forever. We would let the students sleep. Then we would get breakfast. Then we would try to find something to do with them. Some of the students could go out on outings, but not all of them. Also, staffing stopped a few outings. We didn't have enough people to make sure we would all be safe.

We watched videos. We played board games. We ran data driven chores. We talked amongst ourselves.

After working for what felt like fifteen hours, you would look at the wall clock and see that it was just eleven in the morning. Another nine hours to go.

And it was at this time, you would hope for a few restraints to fill up the day. A restraint was a set equation. We didn't want to be in restraints, but we knew what to do in those moments. Restraints meant that there was ten to fifteen minutes of activity followed by paperwork. You have a few more of those, and boy howdy, the shift is over. Sure, you might get injured. You might be filled with fear and trepidation. But at least you were feeling something.

Not a major restraint where the supervisors had to be called. Nothing like that. Just a few run of the mill acting out episodes that necessitated action.

A day with restraints was a day where the after shift beer tasted sweet and satisfying. We always went to a dive bar after the weekend shift. Everyone at the bar avoided us. We were so loud. We told ugly stories about our days and laughed uproariously. We spun tales about our scars like some people tell about the fish that got away. It was that big.

We probably weren't safe to drive home.

10

Bite Guard Malfunction

We had a student who was big and had a reputation for being one of the best biters in the business. She was viscous with her biting. One of the smaller female teachers was petrified of her. She was bitten by the student once and was always trembling when interacting with her.

It came to pass on a weekend that the student was having a bad day. She was screaming and biting her own arm all morning. These were antecedent behaviors that usually lead to an aggressive incident. We used her communication device and offered her preferred items. Nothing was stopping her.

This went on until the middle of the afternoon and we were all on edge. We knew the aggression was coming, but we were exhausted waiting for it. Couldn't she just start it so we could have the restraint and move on with the day?

There had been times when teachers would do or say things they knew would bring out a behavior just to get things to where they were headed. This was never a good idea though. It was just best to wait for the iceberg to hit us.

And finally, it happened. She stopped biting herself. She took a deep breath and charged at one of the teachers. It was the short woman who was afraid of the student. Chris and another teacher jumped in and got her arms. Chris shouted, "Someone get bite."

I was close so I did a bite guard. I said, "Got bite." But I must not have said it loud enough or maybe the short teacher was too freaked out by fear that she didn't hear me. She said, "I'll get bite." She pushed her hand up to secure the chin. By doing this, she dislodged my hand and pushed my fingers up.

My hand was placed right in front of the student's mouth, like we were giving her an offering. The student bit down on my right index finger.

The pain was bright and clear. I screamed at the top of my lungs. I looked at the teeth pushing down on my finger and wondered if I was going to lose it.

Somehow the staff got my finger out. I immediately re-established bite guard.

Someone said, "Dave, you need to break." I waited for someone to take the bite guard from me and I walked back. And that's when I lost my ability to stand. I fell to the floor and my limbs began to shake like I was having a seizure or that I was taken by the spirit at a tent revival.

Eventually, my arms and legs stopped flopping about and I got up and took a deep breath. The restraint was still going on. I watched it from my place on the floor. Tears rushed down my cheeks.

Eventually the student reached calm criteria. She was let go and she was much better for the rest of the day. The short female teacher came up to me later and said that she didn't know I had bite.

"It's okay." It wasn't. I was angry at her. But why bother letting her know? Months later, myself and this teacher found ourselves drunk at a party and we made out like sloppy ships in the night.

11

When to Hold

Every student had a data sheet where we recorded all their important details. For every half hour, we wrote down how many times they hit, or had self-injurious behavior, or spit, or spit at other people, or had a urinary accident (UA) or crapped themselves (BMA) or asked for help or swore. We were constantly making little marks on pages attached to clipboards. Later on, the student's case manager would sum up all these marks and smudges and make graphs. The graphs let someone know if what we were doing was working or not.

Every student had an individual behavior plan. We were expected to know these intimately. These told us what to do for every situation. Or at least, we wished they told us what to do for every situation. How was the student reinforced? What were we to do in case of a targeted behavior? We were not supposed to follow our gut. We were to only respond as the plan told us to. Trust the plan. The plan knows best.

This was also where we knew when to put hands on a student. Each student had a different criterion. It could be, "Three aggressions within thirty seconds." For other students, it would be, "At first aggression." One student might be very difficult to deal with when having a full behavioral incident, so the criteria might read, "If a threatening statement is made, staff will prompt the student to go to the time-out room. If there is an aggression, staff will physically escort student to time out." Doesn't that sound easy? Simple? Usually what occurred was a sped-up film where there were aggressions and staff attempting to walk the thrashing student the ten feet to the time out room. The student would become so aggressive that there would be a restraint on the floor and eventually we would try to pick the student up and carry them to the time out room.

It probably took a minute to write the criteria. It's always easier to write out what is the best procedure. Doing it was always another matter.

But the necessary part was that it was written. It might not make much sense. It might be confusing to follow with fidelity. But it was written. We teachers in jean jackets and baseball caps were followers of the word. The blessed word. We read the behavior plans like scripture. We might debate its liturgical value, but we believed in it all the same.

12

Van Procedures

Transporting to school was challenging. All the students were loaded into two vans. We teachers sat between the students like sea walls. We were there to take the battering waves.

Our team put the kids who had the hardest time in the vans in the back. We always sat next to them waiting for something to happen. The criteria for restraint in the van was strict. If there was any aggression, there was to be a van restraint.

If we were hit by the student, the process was for us to move so that we were on their backs. While doing this we were also pushing their arms forward by the elbows and then we were to wrap the arms across their torso in a basket hold. Then we were to secure the student for the rest of the ten minute van ride. While holding on to their arms crossed over their bellies we would then put our feet on the top of the van and push forward.

This pushed them into their legs. They were crushed forward. They were folded like clams. There was nowhere for them to go. They stayed this way until we reached the school. Then we took our feet off the ceiling of the van and we escorted them to our classroom.

We usually radioed ahead to let them know we were coming in hot. A group of staff were waiting as we pulled into the school parking lot.

And that's how we started the school day.

13
We Did What?

I need to stop this memory of being a kid in his mid-twenties and turn into the middle-aged man I am now. The one who still works with kids on the autism spectrum.

On writing that last chapter about van restraints, I found myself stopping at every sentence and saying to myself, "Holy shit, we did what?"

It goes without saying that this was not a good idea.

It also should be obvious that nothing like that happens now. Well, I hope that something like that doesn't happen now. Or ever.

My excuse is a lame one that doesn't cover an inch of the problem. I was told to do it by a supervisor. It was written in a plan. We did what we were told.

And to make it worse, it was a relief to do that procedure. The van was a dangerous place when a kid acted out. There was no place to run to. We were sitting right there. When I was sitting next to the aggressive student, I just waited for the fist to slam into my face. I waited for the trouble to wake and make its presence known. When we got on the students back and pushed them forward, I knew I was safe. At least for the length of the van ride.

And writing that last paragraph, I find myself ashamed.

14

Another School

In my second year at the school, I found myself going out for a field trip. For one of the special education classes we took at the school, I had to go out and observe another program. There was a well-known school about forty miles away that was having an open house and I went.

This school was known for never using restraints. That's what they said. They had the students do activities and art and they said that solved all problems. I wanted to believe that was true. I wanted to discover that love and kindness was all you needed to work with tough kids. Maybe me and my school had it all wrong.

The open house was very orchestrated. We only saw a few buildings and it culminated in a presentation at the school's auditorium with the entire student body present.

I was up in the balcony with a good amount of people. There were several concerned parents next to me, all wanting the solution to their children's diagnosis.

I was getting bored and my gaze started to check out all the students and staff seated in the front near the stage. I noticed a staff sit down. I think he caught my eye because of the slow, deliberate way he lowered himself into his seat.

The guy had bruises all over his face. One of his eyes was almost closed. His arms had the yellowed circles of skin healing after a bite. I smiled. This guy was my people.

In about three minutes after he sat, other staff went over to him. One of them leaned down and whispered in his ear. The bruised teacher nodded. He got up and quickly left the auditorium, followed by the serious looking staff members.

I couldn't help myself. I had to laugh. Now there was no proof of aggression. Everything was perfect here in the perfect school. I was sure the staff hid that teacher away or sent him home for the day. You can't admit that such things happen.

My laughter made the people close to me annoyed. They gave me looks. I got up and headed home.

15
Break Time

Sometimes, we didn't have it. Sometimes we couldn't secure the arm. Or the kid was twisting his waste and the legs were flapping around. Sometimes the bite guard slipped and the open hand was not covering the jaw but was now around the neck. Sometimes the kid was smarter and angrier and better at this than we were.

That's when we would shout out, "Don't have it."

"I need help on this arm."

"I have it. I lost it."

And chaos would then reign and it didn't look like a well trained unit performing a safety procedure so that no one would get hurt. Sometimes it looked like a drunken rugby scrum done by people who didn't know rugby.

And that's when a smart lead teacher would say the blasted words. They would say, "Break."

Break.

Let go. Get up. Move away. What we were doing was not working. Call it a draw.

Some of us hated when we had to break. We didn't get to calm criteria. We didn't get to a place of safety. The only reason we were doing this was because we didn't do a good enough job.

This was not true. We knew that breaking was about safety. It was about regrouping. If the student was still in a state where aggression would happen, then we would soon enough have another chance to get it right.

But for that first second, when we heard, "Break." It felt like surrender and we were lost in a no man's land, waiting for the next rumblings of war.

And waiting. Waiting was the worst.

16

Sexy Time

Marriages started here. Young people would take this job, this first step in the grown-up world of education. They would get a degree if they took classes provided after their shift. But they also found other young men and women. They fell in love. It makes perfect sense. Who else would understand you and your life? People not working at the school were not to be trusted. They didn't have a clue what things were like.

But for those not inclined for marriage, the restraints could be a little sexy. You are up close with an attractive woman or a good-looking man. If you are on legs, your face is close to the ass of the person on the right arm. You are exerting and putting it all out there.

Sometimes you would stop the serious work of keeping yourself and the student safe and admire the shape of the neck, the exposed ankle of your workmate.

These were people you trusted to keep you safe. And we were all young and in shape. We might say slightly flirty things during the restraint. "Funny running into you."

"We have to stop meeting like this."

Then we would say, while we were writing up the incident, that we should go out for a beer after shift. We needed a beer. No one else can go? Well, then it will just be the two of us.

After a day of keeping each other safe, we looked damned good.

There were times we had to remember that there were students around. Kids who needed us to teach them. Kids who might need to be restrained. If they met criteria.

17

Writing Up

It took skill to write a proper restraint report. You had to remember every detail. You had to go through all the antecedents, all the procedures we did before it reached the time where hands were put on the student.

Everything had to be clear. The supervisor would need to be able to see how it all went down just from what we wrote.

We would start the report with its title. "Three Person Prone Restraint 12 minutes." Or "One person basket hold, standing, for 3 minutes."

Then the details. We would not skimp on anything. Except for emotion. There were no deep feelings in these accounts. No one thought anything or felt anything. We were dispassionate.

At least on the page.

18

What Monsters We Were

We were horrible at parties. We made people at the bar uncomfortable. Our laughter was always two notches above everyone else's.

We told amusing anecdotes. Like how I got this scar on my finger. Or how Sheila's hat was eaten by a student. Or Chris would tell the time that we had to go home dressed in clothes leant to us by our very own students. We were covered in shit and blood that day.

That was how these drunken sessions of confessions and alibis went. All the stories were covered in shit and blood.

19

That Afternoon

I was there that day. The day you heard of. I was there.

I was with my student, heading to the van in the school's parking lot. The school day was over and now we had a trip to the residence. My student was on edge that day. I was focusing on his large hands. Hoping they would stay by his side. I wanted peace today. I wanted an easy afternoon.

As we quickly headed to the van, I noticed a bunch of staff restraining a student on the asphalt. It was the team for the little kids. They all had on their professional faces. I felt for them. It was always a bummer having to restrain right before you got to the van. I moved on. I had my student.

Had I known that things were going terribly wrong in that restraint, would I have done anything differently? Probably not. I had my own student to worry about.

The next day, we were told that the team for the little kids needed people to take overtime shifts. Any time we could give for that team, it would be great. And it was overtime pay.

I signed up for a few asleep overnight shifts. Only then did I ask Chris why they needed the staffing.

"Dude? Where have you been? You remember that restraint we passed yesterday?"

"We pass a lot of restraints."

"The one in the parking lot. The kid was on his stomach. He asphyxiated. He died."

It was somber working at that residence that week. It was somber everywhere.

And that's what I remember from that afternoon. People in the field bring it up. They mention that there have been a few deaths during restraints in the state. They mention that one. Sometimes I say, I was there. Sometimes I just keep quiet.

20

My Shoulder

Every morning, my shoulder reminds me of my three years at the school. For the past six months, I wake up uncomfortable. My shoulder throbs me awake. My range of motion in that arm is not as good as it used to be. And the pain in the morning allows me to feel older than I am.

Almost a quarter century since I left that job and it pokes at me every day.

The wear and tear of the job did a number on my shoulder and in my third year at the school, it was so bad, I had to go to the doctor. He said it was sore and inflamed. I was to wear a sling for a week, to rest the shoulder.

The job expected me there anyway. I was on light duty, no restraints. The sling was an invitation to the students to go after me. It was a long week. I was more battered at the end of my time with the sling then I was before it.

I learned to ignore the shoulder. There was always Tylenol and a shot of whiskey when I got home. There are always remedies for such things.

I am still in the field. Special Education. I still work with challenging students. And things have improved. We do not do what we were once allowed to. And that's a blessing. Things head in the right direction.

Recently, I was in a meeting with a support staff. He complained that things are awful now. We are not allowed to do the smart things anymore. We can't wrap up a kid and take them out of class. We are all too nice now. We can't get anything done because we are just too sweet and useless.

The man who said it was my age, but he looked older than me. I wonder if his shoulder is hurting him too.

21
The One I Recall

I have this ability of forgetting most of the students I have worked with. Not really forgetting, but I can put them aside. It allows me to focus on the current students. The past is just that. Most teachers are not like that. They keep certain kids close to their hearts. The one that touched them. The ones that they made a difference for.

Not me. The only one I hold close is a student from that school. She came my second year. She was as sweet and gentle as a kitten. Great kid. I liked her a lot. But we didn't have time to really spend with her. The non-violent kids were left alone a lot as we dealt with the aggressive ones. We made sure they were set and then ran off to help in the restraint.

We never meant to have it occur, but we ignored her. Because she was sweet. Because she was easy.

She had her first aggression about five months into her time with us. All of us were flabbergasted. We couldn't figure out what was going on.

This was not a blip. This continued. This increased. By the time I left that team and went to another residence for my final year, she was an aggressive student with her very own behavior plan and an individualized criteria for restraint and for calm. She had moved up in the world. She had gotten the attention that was deprived her. Eventually, her parents had enough and had her removed.

We made her.

We had many, many successes with our students. But I don't remember them. I remember the failure we created. The one I keep close to my heart.

22

A Line from a Poem

A few years ago, I accompanied my wife to a youth poetry event in the city. This was a slam poetry competition where different schools competed with their own poetry. My wife was coaching the team for the school she taught at.

I was on my own for a little bit and got to watch a bout between four schools. One girl came up on stage. By the way her body listed to one side, it was evident that she had some physical disability. She was a slight thing and the microphone stand towered over her.

She adjusted the microphone confidently. She spoke her first line with conviction. "The kids in my special ed class would take bets on who would be restrained most that day."

The poem went on, and I struggled to hear it all. I was gut punched.

I was hearing what the students felt, at last. I was hearing the rebuttal.

A restraint robs the person of the ability to move freely. And that's what we did. But I forgot to think about how the student felt about it. We only did it because we needed them and others to be safe.

And yet, this line from this poem made me realize that they mocked us. They found us ridiculous.

I couldn't disagree.

Completed at 10:15 on Thursday January 21, 2021.

How to Write a Memoir in Three Days: A Memoir

Started March, 12, 2021 at 6PM
Slide One
How to Write a Memoir in Three Days

This is the moment where I get up from my seat in the front row and take the podium. I smile slightly uncomfortably, as if to say, "I don't know exactly what I am doing, but here we go and I might as well try my damnedest to make this thing work.

The first slide is projected on the screen and I look at it with you, as if I was not the person to create it. Like I am just seeing this for the first time.

When I do powerpoint presentations, I am one who always reads what is on the screen as if it is holy text. Like I am reading it for a group of people who might be illiterate so I feel the need to read it out for them.

I will say out loud, "How to Write a Memoir in Three Day." I am about to say more, but realize that the microphone is not working and no one can hear me. "Can you hear me?" is greeted with blank, bored expressions. I play with the microphone and wonder why no one can hear me. I am getting a little annoyed and my cool is totally blown. The microphone is shot. I have useless equipment.

A tech guy comes and he looks even more annoyed than me and asks me if I actually turned the mic on and I tell him that of course I turned it on, how crazy do you think I am. Then the tech guy leans over and turns the mic on and everyone can hear me.

I think about running out of the room and breaking down into embarrassed tears, but the ham in me reappears and reminds me that the show must go on. Actually, the show must start. And so it will. I start talking. Which is one of my favorite things in the world to do.

When I am in front of a group of people I always am freaked out. Am I prepared enough? Do I have enough slides to fill up the time I have been given? What if everyone in the room is bored out of their mind? Will I overcompensate and start shouting and swearing and being out there just to get people's attention?

Powerpoint presentations are the worst thing that ever happened to discourse. There was a time in the 19th century when going to a lecture was a big entertainment. People loved going to these things. They went to them like we go to the movies or see a band. It was the cool thing to do. I imagine people getting concert t-shirts for the Ralph Waldo Emerson lecture they saw in Harford. Or those who were trading in bootleg wax cylinders of Mark Twain's talk at the Elk's Club 1903, which is far superior to the one he gave in 1904.

But concerts and flicks killed that kind of fun. Now going to a lecture is a chore. It's work. And most of the time it is for work. It is a requirement. It is something you have to do instead of want to do.

And when the powerpoint was introduced everything went to hell. Now everyone has all their information on slides. Bleached of any flair or nuance. You see someone set up the computer to present their Powerpoint and you can feel your soul flatten.

I am a Behavior Analyst for my job and it turns out that I have given a lot of work required lectures. How to give reinforcement. What is the best way to teach a behavior chain. What are the four functions of behavior.

These are the things I have been creating and teaching to staff who really could care less. I actually like doing them and try to make them funny. The jokes I include are intended to make me laugh and no one else. I am a selfish lecturer that way. But I guess it works, because I have heard one of the staff ask, "Is this another Story Time With Dave?"

I was tickled when I heard that because a lecture should be a story. It should be fun. Yes, you are getting information, but let's not make this shit dull. I remember reading somewhere that you should have no more than 20 slides. The idea being that you should have everything refined and clear. You can talk around the 20 slides. You can fill in the spaces. Give it your personality. If you have one.

Feeling like I have dawdled enough, I begin.

Hi. Thank you all for coming. My name is David Macpherson and I have found myself being a memoirist. In the past year I have written five of these little darlings.

There was <u>My Life in the Frank N Furter Cult.</u> About my misspent youth going to The Rocky Horror Picture Show.

Next was <u>Walking and Reading,</u> which, surprise surprise, is about just that. My love of reading books while walking. Though I think more than half of it dealt with the time a car hit me while I was walking and reading.

The third memoir from this year was <u>Vultures, Vultures Everywhere.</u> That was about seeing the movie Casablanca in a theater during the Covid outbreak. It also went over my love of moviegoing. In all fairness, that one didn't work out well. But i will talk about that later, because failures are so much more interesting than successes.

The fourth has the unwieldy title of <u>Adrift on the Lost Channels: A Love Story of the 1970s.</u> Wow. I had to look it up to remember what it's called. This was about my love of cheesy TV shows that I watched as a kid on UHF channels. It also is a look at how I handled or didn't handle the death of my father. Yeah, memoirs can be tricky things. You think you are reading a funny book about watching Speed Racer, and wham. The kid's dad dies.

The last of the five memoirs is the shortest one, but it might mean the most to me. <u>The Criteria for Calm.</u> That one is my memories about being a young special education teacher in a challenging school and the need to restrain the students when they became violent. I know, a fun topic. But we will go over that later, as well.

What makes these five short books worth mentioning? Because all of them were written in three days. None of them took more than 72 hours to complete. It was a challenge I set up for myself. Write a book in three days.

I am now a huge fan and believer in this process. That's why i am conducting this lecture, because I think this is something you can do as well. You might be surprised by what you can create in just three days.

But i should warn you. This is not a simple tutorial. This is not a bare bones look at the process of how to do it. No, my friends. This is also....

I take a long dramatic pause and press the button to go to the second slide. Nothing happens. God, I suck at technology. I realize that I am pressing the wrong button. I press the right one, and we are off and running.

Boy, this was a lot longer a dramatic pause than I hoped for.

Slide 2
How to Write a Memoir in Three Days
A Memoir

I read this out loud and give extra emphasis on the "A memoir" part expecting a laugh. I am not quite sure why I expect that this is a laugh line, but I thought it was funny and I am soaking in wishful thinking. It does not get much of anything. Maybe there was a titter in the back row, but that could be two people telling something funny to each other.

Right, this is a memoir as well. If we are talking about writing a memoir, then we should make that about memory as well. There is a reason I wrote all of these pieces in three days. There is a story behind it. There is a story behind all the decisions that I made. Won't that be a piece of my life that I am sharing? Isn't that what a memoir is?

Actually, that is a great question. What is a memoir? I am not kidding. I really don't know. I have no idea what it is. What is the difference between a memoir, an autobiography or a factual retelling? I am sure that smarter people than me can give you an idea of what shape each of these things are.

I remember reading a memoir by Samuel Delaney and he defined that it wasn't over long or dry. But you might read his book and feel that it is overlong. I don't personally think that, but I am sure that someone picked up the revised edition and thought to themselves, "Too many words."

Let's just try to define it for now. A memoir is a book that tells a story of your life. It might be a long tale full of intrigue and plot points. It might be a small memoir about meeting a famous person or an important day in your life.

This is the cool and difficult part of memoir, it is what you say it is. It is all of these things. Now most of my three day memoirs are short. They are around 10 thousand words in length. Around forty pages or so. The last one was just 7 thousand words. I didn't run out of time with that one. I just said everything I wanted to say and realized I was done.

But some people might not want to call such a small thing a book. They might say it is a novelette sized memoir.

Those are just ridiculous terms. It is a book because I say it is. It is a memoir for the same reason.

You are a writer not because you have a truckload of accolades. You don't get a writer's license. You are a writer because you say so. So much of this writing schtick is poise and bullshit. Your work is the right length for what you are making. You are writing a memoir because that's what you wrote.

Don't say, "I'm trying to be a writer." Don't say, "I just am waiting to hear from my writing mentor to see if I should continue with this book." You are a writer. You should continue.

The important part is to write. Just write. You will get better. I feel like each writing project I do allows me to improve. Sometimes I don't make the book work, but that is worthwhile because it allows me to think of what went wrong and try again.

Okay. I think we have had enough of the rah-rah I am a writer, you are a writer cheerleading.

I mean, it is important to have the cheerleading. It is important to know that you are allowed to create what you want.

But we have a lot to go over.

And we are just on the second slide.

Slide Three
The Origin of the Three Day Memoir

This is the part that is pure memoir. This is about me and my life. Like I said. There is no way you can avoid it.

This starts with Covid. Like a lot of things. Covid started a lot. It started insecurity and isolation. But it also allowed art minded people to create. And that's what happened to me.

The schools were closed, but in that first week, the stores were still open. I went to the comic shop to stock up on old weird comics, figuring that this pandemic would be over in a few weeks (yeah, we were all so naive and optimistic).

While I was there I noticed they had the latest issue of the long running zine Cometbus. Aaron Cometbus has been putting out his zine about living the punk life for something like 30 years. He puts out about one issue a year. Each issue tells one story. Some of them are fiction, but most of them are memoir or reporting. One of them was a collection of interviews with comic book creators. Another was a memory of buying and selling books in New York. I love them. When I see a new issue, I stop all my other reading and plunge into it. They are about 100 pages and I am usually done in a few days. Which is sad, because then I have another year until he writes and puts out the next issue.

Because he makes it himself, the cost is cheap. The latest issue was five dollars. As I purchased it, I thought that was one of the best things about DIY zine making, they go right from the writer to the reader. It is direct. And it is cheap. I have always believed in cheap books for the people.

I put out one or two eBooks of my stuff every month and part of my ethic is that they are always on the low end of the price range. My books are short, so I can't justify giving them a high price tag. They range from 99 cents to 2.99. I put out a large 300 page book about going to every bar in Worcester and having one gin and tonic at each place. I charged 3.99. People thought I was crazy. I should value my work more and give it a higher price tag.

The thing is, I value you the idea of affordable words most.

And in that way, I was inspired by the issue of Cometbus that I was reading. I was walking the dog a lot, being that I wasn't going to my job. The schools I was working in were closed. So the dog was getting insanely long walks and I was reading the zine. I was thinking, "I want to do something like this. I want to create a fast zine." The dog was thinking, "When are these crazy people going to go back to work and leave me in peace?"

On the Thursday of the first week without school, I had to drive to my son's school to pick up school work for him. We live an hour from the school, so I had a lot of time to listen to the car radio and all the doom telling. I even stopped at a supermarket looking for toilet paper and butter. I found the butter, but no toilet paper. Everyone had decided that the only way to survive a pandemic was to horde toilet paper.

While waiting in line with my purchases, I checked my phone and noticed that a guy who ran a press and who published some of my work in the past, was announcing that he had just put together an eZine. It was free to download because it was all just images he took from the internet. I downloaded it and was assaulted by images of scantily clad women sporting vampire teeth. That was the zine, pictures of women dressed up as sexy vampires.

What the hell?

This was not what I was hoping for, but I still dug the idea that he was bored so he put out a zine. A silly zine with questionable taste, sure, but he threw it together and it was out in the world for people to look at.

And it was that and the Cometbus issue that made me realize that I needed to put out a monthly eZine. I had already learned how to make covers and format eBooks. I was ready to go. I just needed an idea. Which I didn't have.

I got to the school, picked up my son's work and started driving home.

On the drive home, still listening to NPR, I was amused by the fear and panic everyone was going through. That I was going through. I suddenly remembered the old book 1001 Ways to Avoid the Draft. It was a classic anti-war book. I thought I should do that. I should do 1001 Things to Do While Sitting Out a Pandemic.

While still driving home, I played with the idea and realized that I could do it, but I knew full well that I was not going to come up with 1001 ideas. I just wasn't that clever. My solution was that I would write this thing for three days and when the time was up, the book was done. I would title it the number I got to in that time.

That seemed like a good strategy and I was still psyched and I would start as soon as I got home. And as I was congratulating myself, I was thinking bigger. This was how I was going to do a monthly eZine. I would do a book every month in three days. That would be the hook. 72 hours for a book. I soon thought that I should have other writers I know do this. I am part of a strong writing scene in Worcester, so I had people to invite. Who knows what the books would be, just that they would be done in 3 days.

I did the book and got it done at the wire of 72 hours. It was called <u>367 Things to Do While Sitting Out a Pandemic.</u> It's alright as far as list books go. For some reason, it is my bestselling eBook. I needed to give the zine a name and I waited until the last possible second to come up with a title. I used to run a poetry reading called the Hangover Hour Spoken Word Salon. I thought Hangover Hour is the best title for almost anything, so I named the zine the Hangover Hour Report.

Then my friend Jeff Campbell took up my challenge and wrote a long fiction story and it was good and that was my second issue.

Then it was my time to come up with the third issue. I figured I would do it and I picked memoir. Here is my feeling about memoir and why many people write them. You don't have to create anything new or do a lot of research. You can just remember something and write. In that way it is easy. Or, as least, it seems easy.

Slide Four

The First Three Day Memoir

On the slide is a picture of the cover to the Hangover Hour Issue Three. This is the one that means the most to me, so I pause and just let people bask in the greatness of it. It's pretty cool cover where the Rocky Horror Picture Show singing lips is shown as a simple icon.

Okay. Here it is. <u>My Life in the Frank N Furter Cult.</u> Like a lot of these little three day memoirs, they have all been things I have thought about writing. But in the past, I have been bogged down with how to do it and how much prep work will it entail. Also, there was always the fear that I wouldn't have enough story or memory to fill up a whole book.

I think I decided to do this book when I was watching YouTube videos of a particular good live stage version of the Rocky Horror Show. The band was amazing and the singers were strong and I suddenly thought back to all my old Rocky Horror days. In the back of my mind was the nagging thought that I had to come up with a topic for my next three day zine. And like that, I had the idea and the title.

I was working remotely, slowly losing my mind, and I waited to write the book on my April vacation. April vacation was a lot like every other week while living in Pandemic World. I planned on what day I was going to start. I set up at the dining room table and started. I trudged through.

Now what I said a few minutes ago, that memoir is easy because there is no research involved is kind of bullshit. You have to remember things. You have to verify your recollection with friends or documents. You have to tell the story with enough detail that it isn't a weak memory. You don't want your memoir to sound like your Uncle Stu telling a joke, where the punchline is said first and all the set up is off.

I did the research while writing. I wanted a little more detail about the origin of Rock Horror and how it became a midnight movie sensation and I found wonderful articles online. I wanted to talk to my friend Foster, who was there during all the Rocky years, and I DMed him and he gave such good answers I put them in the book.

I guess what I am saying is that the internet makes writing the three day memoir possible. You need a quote or some information from someone, you can get it without a long trip to the library or a long distance phone call. And what you can't find, don't worry, I'm sure you didn't need to impart that much detail.

I'm not kidding about that. Sometimes we writers get lost in the minutiae. We spend days searching for a small piece of information. I am here to tell you, that you probably didn't need that. And if you did find the information, would it's inclusion bog down the forward movement of the story? Probably.

I loved writing this piece. I was excited to sit down and tackle it. I was shocked when it turned into what it really was about. One of my high school friends was Tommy who died of cancer at the age of 45. He was a great, large soul. He was happy and adventurous and I was lucky to know him. He was a major figure in my time going to Rocky Horror and soon I realized that I was writing a memoir about our friendship..

I didn't know that was what the book was going to be. It just happened. I was smart enough to not do any course correction. I let the book turn into something I had not planned and I was so happy.

When I got to writing about his death, I kept it simple. I was surprised by how short that chapter was. I was honest, but I kept it brief. It was hard to write, but it was written quickly. Like pulling off a band-aid.

I was proud of it. But the amazing part was that Foster gave copies of the eBook to Tommy's family. His sister and his mother both read it and liked it. His mother wrote me a thank you note. She was honored that I wrote about her son with such love. I was gutted and proud.

Last week, I read my own book. This is something I do not do. Once I am done with a book, I am done. I am thinking about what I am going to write next. But I saw a print copy of it in a bookcase and

I read the whole thing while standing. And I must say that this little book that I wrote in three days is the best thing I have ever done. I am pleased to have created it.

And part of the reason it turned out well is because I only gave myself three days to do it. I didn't have the time to worry about it. I didn't have the time to wonder if I got the right balance or if I should go back and work on that section. No time. I had to be done in 72 hours.

There have been twelve issues of the zine. I changed the name of it at the fourth issue because I was proud of what I was producing and the Hangover Hour Report was a dumb name. One guy I approached to write an issue said he might do it when he has a long weekend. And that's how the zine changed its name to The Long Weekend Review.

I think this process opened me up as a writer. It allowed me to not worry and just write. To trust my writing and my memory. The speed of it is one of the best parts. And I think it can do wonders for other writers.

Slide Five

But Wait....We Have Testimonials!

If I am going to sell the audience with my vision of Three Day Memoirs, then I better show that it isn't just me. This is tough, because the two writers I got to sing the praises of the process are so much better writers than me. I am almost afraid to bring them on, for making me look bad. I take out the written pages and hope to hell that I have enough light to read them. I find my reading glasses in the wrong pocket, but at least I found them.

In the course of the year span I put out The Long Weekend Review, I invited other writers to try to do it. I told them that they can write whatever they want. I was lucky enough to get four talented writers. I knew them all from the poetry scene in Worcester. They were all regulars at the open mic I run. Most of what they wrote were memoir-like. David Jahn did a wonderful piece about the state of the world we are in now and the idea of trying to go back to normal. Katie Elizabeth wrote about her experience dealing with chronic fatigue syndrome. I was unable to get in touch with them in time, but I was able to hear what the Campbells felt about writing these fast memoirs.

Gwyneth Campbell was only 19 when she started going with her Dad to the poetry reading I run. I asked her to write a book in three days and she came back from college and knocked it out of the park. First, she wrote the longest book in the series. She wrote about her struggles with special needs and how the school system interacted with her. It is amazing and fierce. It is called <u>Second Hand Bodies and One Winged Butterflies.</u> I consider this the best book in the series.

This is what she wrote to me. "Without the time constraint I would have spent every moment thinking and analyzing every little scene. It would have lost some of the organic nature, I think. Things would have been replaced with attempts for perfection and trying to sound profound. The book was definitely something I thought about writing, but held back because it always felt harder to write about. Add on to the fact that with being only 21, anytime I would mention wanting to write about my experiences, I got a lot of "you're too young, wait until you have more" so i kept holding off writing it because it felt like even if I would write it, no one would listen. Parts of my story were so vulnerable and angry I needed an invitation to tell them, because writing that part of my story and having no one listen would have really messed with my head. I am 100% surprised I got that much written. i didn't notice how much it was until the end. I had completely been prepared to have the shortest one and was worried I wasn't going to write enough for it to be published. It became me needing to prove not just to others but myself that i had done something worth writing and that I could have enough to write about."

I hold up the piece of paper for the audience to see as if to prove that there are actual words there and I didn't make the whole thing up.

Gwyn's dad is Jeff Campbell and is also a poet. He has published several books about his Christian faith and meditation. I thought it would be great to see what he could do with the three day time limit. He wrote the second issue, which was a science fiction story. I encouraged him to try to write about his faith and he came up with <u>A Whole Lot of Nothing,</u> which was the seventh issue. I really like this book. He goes deeply in his faith, but also the issues he has with it.

Here is what Jeff wrote. "Well, going in I knew I wanted it to be about my spirituality. But writing about all the things that are going well is boring and also makes it look like you want to convert people. And honestly, I couldn't give two shits about convincing somebody I am right. So I knew even before I started that it had to be about some aspect of my spirituality that was more of a struggle. So I knew I was going to want to be real and authentic, and even a little bit raw. But I didn't really grasp how much the format was going to help that. When you've got the luxury of time, you end up having the ability to talk yourself into things and out of things. There's time to justify and rationalize and make deals with yourself. To fluff and finesse. Normal writing is almost like the version of you that can be presented on social media. It's curated, prefabricated. Having just a single weekend to write the thing, I occupied the whole of my head space with just the act of writing. I wasn't tempted, I don't think, to stop and alter things; I was so busy pushing forward into whatever kind of territory was next I didn't allow myself to turn around. And rewrite the past passages. So I think it was one of the most authentic things I've ever written."

Wow. The three day memoir can give you authenticity.

In all seriousness, being able to get others to try this challenge and to have them all write fine work was the biggest honor for me.

So now you are interested in how to do this three day memoir. My simple advice is to say, just do it. Sit down and start writing. In three days, stop.

But that's not great advice. It might be true, but the idea of writing a whole piece in three days can be daunting. So, let's go through a few suggestions. Some rules of the road. These are things that have worked for me in getting these completed. You might like what I suggest and try it, or might just go your own way. That's cool. I am not asking you to write like me. How boring a world we have if everyone writes in the same way?

Slide Six

Step One - Pick a Topic You are Interested but isn't so Large or Vast that You will be Overwhelmed.

How did I come up with these ideas for my little memoirs? Well, I thought of something, like going to Rocky Horror or watching bad TV on UHF stations when I was a kid or the act of walking and reading. I might think that this is something I would like to write about. In two of the memoirs, I tried in the past to write about the subject and then got stymied. I wrote something like 8000 words about walking and reading and it just kept on going and I kept losing my focus. Eventually, I abandoned it. I thought of it again and said to myself, "Why don't I try to do it in three days?" And with that question asked, the whole thing falls into place.

I never said, "I want to write a three day memoir, what topic can I use?" It was always the other way around. I came up with a topic and only then did I consider putting it on a time clock.

I wouldn't pick a topic that is really tough. I wouldn't say, "Now I want to write about my relationship with my abusive family." There is nothing wrong about writing that. But it is heavy. For writing in three days, you can pick a neutral topic, like all the things you cooked in the kitchen when you were a kid, and the tough topics will show up. That's how I would do it. I know the Campbells, from the last slide, tackled hard topics right from the start. That's how they write.

For me, I like to wander into the tough things. I wrote about the death of a friend through a book about Rocky Horror. My book about watching bad TV became an examination about the early death of my father. I wrote about my habit of reading books while walking the dog and most of that was about the time a car hit me and all the trauma that brought. Watching the movie Casablanca was my attempt to come to grips with the pandemic we are still in.

All of this is how I do it. I pick a general topic and wonder if there is enough to hang words on. If it is a sturdy topic, I then find three days to write it. I trust myself that real emotion will appear.

The first time I was aware of the arbitrary aspect of memoir was back in high school when I discovered Spalding Gray. He was a monologuist who told stories about his life. A friend lent me a collection of his early monologues. One of them was called "Sex and Death to the Age of 14." Everything about the monologue was in the title. He compiled all his experiences with sex and death until he was 14 years old. He put it together and that was his spoken word memoir. You can do it that way. "Every time I was embarrassed at a shopping mall." "My first 50 kisses."

Your job before the clock starts is to think about all of those instances that fit your theme. You will worry about meaning later. The act of writing will create the meaning. Now, you don't have to keep the title. The title is the least important part of this process. It can help you define what you are writing, and then you can change it. When I first started <u>The Criteria for Calm</u> it had a terrible title, "Restraining Other People." Man, did that ever blow. But that's what the book was about, it was about the weird process of restraining violent students. I tacked that title on and knew it was probably temporary. The writing was going along and I started talking about the criteria the student has to reach for them to be considered to be calm and for the restraint to be over. I wrote down in one chapter, "He had not reached his criteria for calm." And I stopped typing and realized that I found the title for the book.

You might not listen to me and decide to go for the pressing, and difficult, topic for your book. That's fine. But remember, you are going to be flying along with this story. Will you be able to write such a book? That's up to you. In some ways, the three day memoir might be the best way to tackle it, because you are not going to be spending weeks or months reliving this story. In this way, you have three days and then you are done. It's ripping off the band-aid.

Slide Seven
Step Two - Find the Time to Do It

One of the reasons that I have not gotten people to write three day memoirs is because they can't find the time to commit to it. That's fine. It is one reason that I am ending the zine. I figured I would write every second or third book, but now I have written the last five. It is just me. I am doing it, I have been successful getting a book every month, but I don't know if people want issue after issue of just me.

I have been able to find the time. I like to go away and write at hotels. Three of these have been written at the Latchis Hotel in Brattleboro, Vermont. I like it there and can focus.

The first one I wrote at the dining room table at home. I knew for a week the day I was going to start writing. I made an appointment. I let my family know that I was going to get started on it.

For <u>Adrift on the Lost Channels</u> I wrote it in between work and a class I was taking. It was not ideal, but the book worked out okay. I came up with the idea for the memoir and I was really jazzed to do it. I was very excited for it. I did my research about the old TV shows I used to watch and I couldn't wait. I didn't have any real time to get away, so I just decided to start it on Friday night and work around the family commitments. It turned out certain obligations took precedence and I didn't get going until Sunday morning.

But I wanted to write it. So I just plowed through. I found an hour here, a half hour there. I set my alarm for five in the morning and wrote for two hours on Monday and Tuesday mornings. My enthusiasm for the work allowed me to find the time to get it finished. And it turned out as good as I could get it. Two days later, I had a cover for it and I had set it up as an eBook. From the time I had the idea to write the book until it was available for sale online was eight days. That is so cool.

Now, I should warn you that life can happen and you will not finish the book in the three days. And that's fine. That's more than fine. Let's say it takes you an extra three days to get it done. Well, that's awesome. You just wrote a memoir in six days.

Or you have to put it down for a week and finish it later. That's fine too. But you wrote it. You finished it.

There might be a time where you give it your all and you just don't think it's working. I will talk more about that later, but my feeling is that you just give it your best try. If you didn't finish the book, think of this as practice. Think of this as an opportunity to learn how you are as a writer. So you don't have a finished memoir, but you are working at the writing and that will do nothing but improve your skills for the next time.

Slide Eight

Step Three - Make a Little List

On the slide is a picture of an envelope with some of my unwieldy handwriting on it. See. I can mix it up. I have included a picture on the slide. I am embracing technology, I am a force to be reckoned with.

This is the list for my book on old TV programs. Before I started, I wrote down the titles of what I wanted to talk about. There are a few other things I put on the list so I don't forget. While I am writing, I have the list next to me. If I'm not sure where to go next, I take a look at it.

I don't do outlines. I just write and see where I go. All I have is the list, which is more a prompt than anything else. Sometimes I look at the list and decide that I don't want to write about the item. The story I am telling might have veered into a different direction and the list is now superfluous.

When I was writing <u>Walking and Reading</u> the list was pretty long. I had a lot of things I knew I wanted to include. The funny thing is, sometimes the thing on the list turned out to be just a few sentences. Other times, I realized I covered that already and I can cross it out. When I was all done with the book, I looked at the list and realized that I forgot to include a few things I thought were necessary. But the book turned out fine without these things.

That's a nice thing about writing quickly, you are just moving forward and if you forgot to include something, then maybe it's your writing brain telling you that it was not important to include.

This little to-do list of memoir writing allows you to be flexible. It allows you to discover what the book wants to be. If you are forcing every detail and thought into it, then the book will be airless and overstuffed. We are making fleet books here.

Once again, not writer writes exactly alike. This works for me. It might work for you.

Slide Nine

Step Four - Be True Instead of Factual

Be true instead of factual. What the hell do I mean? I mean be honest in your writing, but don't worry about getting every detail exactly the way it happened.

We are still trying to write a story here. I have no problem with streamlining things. I only have three days, I don't have time to write all the conversation I had with a person. I'm just going to consolidate it into one.

I will change a few things here and there, just because it reads better.

Don't be bogged down with getting everything perfect. The hell with perfect. I am sure you might have heard someone say that a piece of dialogue isn't working and the writer will complain and say, "But that is exactly what the person said." That's being factual. The thing is, you should rewrite it so it's better on the page.

When I wrote <u>The Criteria for Calm</u> I had to change a lot of things. I wanted to talk about that time in my life, but I also wanted to be respectful to those who were there. It was easier to change details and names. Was the book factual? No. But I am proud that it expressed something I believed to be true. In the front of the book, I did say that events and people had been altered. I am not trying to fool anyone.

Memoir has a history of fabrication. There are the people who said they were in a gang, when they were not. There was the memoir of a woman surviving the Holocaust that was completely made up.

I am not talking about that. Please don't do that. Change a few things to move the story along. Don't make shit up. It not only makes your book untreatable, it also muddies the water for the rest of us. We get the stink on us by association.

And you know, if you want to make up cool things, then just write it as a novel. It can be based on your life, but you changed a lot. And if you call it a novel, then you can write it the way you want it to be. But if you are saying it is a memoir, try to be true to the events that you are relaying.

Slide Ten

Step Five -Forgive Your Mess Ups

Here is a truth about my books. The first chapter is always the weakest. I am not saying that they are bad, but compared to later chapters, they are weak. As I move on in a three day memoir, the chapters get shorter and punchier. I am feeling the time and I want to get to the end. I want to get to the good parts, so I ignore a lot of the other details.

This makes sense because every time you write a piece, you are learning what the book is. The first chapter is a first date. You two are just getting to know each other.

Now, when I have written novels and realize the first chapter isn't up to the rest, I might rewrite it. I don't do a lot of rewrites, but if the beginning isn't working at all compared to the rest, I will try to fix it.

But with this three day challenge, I might look at the first chapter and say good enough. I don't have the time for a well reasoned overhauling. I just let it go. For the most part, it is enough.

I am not saying that you can write crap. I am just saying trying for perfection is boring and time consuming.

Forgive your mistakes. Just move on. Think of everything you write as practice for the next thing you write. You will improve. This challenge might help you improve.

While writing my fourth memoir, I was also posting my word count progress on Facebook. I got some encouragement, and that's nice. One person was not so nice. He asked, "Who cares about how many words you wrote. What if they are the wrong words? What if you are writing badly. It doesn't matter how many words you write if all of them are bad."

Somehow I found it in myself not to tell him to screw off. Instead I wrote, "That's okay. If it isn't good, then I will say I was just practicing. Just learning to find those good words."

I got the concept that writing can be practice from a fine author and teacher named Dean Wesley Smith. As soon as I heard the idea, I became a better writer.

I used to write about once a week. That was my routine. I now write every day. My personal rule is that as long as I write at least 200 words a day, then I have written. 200 words a day is only like ten or fifteen minutes. It is not a lot, but 200 words a day will get you a novel in under a year. And it is practice. I am getting an opportunity to work at writing.

And sometimes what I write doesn't work. That's okay. I'll write something else next time. And don't forget to read a lot. Think about how the writer you just read got her thoughts to you. Study. Read about writing. Don't always believe what the writing professionals tell you. Be critical.

Even me, don't trust me either. Well trust me when I say that it is better to try to write a great book and come up short then not writing it. Okay, the book was not a masterpiece, but it is pretty good. You succeeded in writing a good book. Awesome.

That's why the three day memoir is great for me. I just wrote and didn't worry about the mistakes or the fact that it isn't perfect. It is the best I could do.

Does that mean all my books are good? Oh, no.

Let me tell you about my third three day memoir.

Let me tell you about.....

I take a long pause, because I love the drama of withholding the next slide. I now press the button and away we go.

Slide Eleven

Vultures, Vultures Everywhere! - A Case Study

This was the third I did. And I was trying to do something different. I was challenging myself with this one. And the challenge beat me.

Last June, I was up at Brattleboro writing what was to be <u>Walking and Reading.</u> The hotel I stay at has an old school movie theater on the first floor. The weekend I was there was the first one where they were going to show movies again. Things up in Vermont were opening up slightly. But there were no new movies being released, so they were showing Casablanca. A classic movie in an old movie palace. I could not miss that.

My wife said that it might be interesting if I write about going back to the movies. I thought so too, so I started taking notes.

When I got to writing it, it was July. I found a long weekend where I could watch the movie and do it. I also decided to focus on the actor who played the pickpocket in Casablanca. That actor was also in a wonderful German movie called Wings of Desire.

So my idea was to weave in Casablanca, Wings of Desire and my memories of movie going. I also thought that I should try to do it in a different way. I was going to have short little paragraphs and that a lot of it will be quotes from the movies and other places. I thought that it might feel like a collage where I am using my own story, as well as lines from the movies to create a rich tapestry..

The writing was tough. I had problems settling on what tense I was going to use. I kept on flipping from past tense to present tense. Writing down all the quotes was a chore. I didn't know if the very idea of quotes interspersed with personal recollection made any sense. I finished it in under three days and then I looked at it. I don't think it came out well. My attempt to try something different was admirable, but I didn't pull it off. I even thought about not putting it out.

But I did put it out. I spent the time creating something. I might be wrong about it. Other people might like it. And more than that, all of these little books are just part of a process. They are all part of my development in the craft of writing. And part of that process is allowing other people the chance to read it. Also, I didn't worry too long over it, because I was busy writing the next thing.

Did I learn anything from <u>Vultures! Vultures Everywhere</u>? Very much so. I learned to make sure I had a plan for tense. That this type of book might work, but probably not under a tight deadline. I also had to have a better idea of structure before I started. These are all good things to know. You don't know any of it if you don't try.

Failures happen. But not every time.

Slide Twelve
Step Six - Don't Dawdle. Finish the Book.

One of the amazing things is when I am writing these memoirs, I am shocked when the ending shows up. For the one about watching UHF TV shows I knew what the last line was. I just needed to get there. For the others, I was always surprised. I would finish the chapter and realize, oh, that's the end.

For the most part, these are all short. You have three days, most of them will be around 10 to 20 thousand words. For <u>The Criteria for Calm</u> I thought it was going to be long because I thought had a lot of story to tell. But it turned out to be seven thousand words. That's it. I got to the end a lot sooner than I planned. But it was all I wanted it to be.

I know we all like big fat books, but telling a story well and completely is even better. I have always liked short books. I love the idea of sitting down for an afternoon and finishing a book. Cover to cover. Now that there is eBooks, I feel that it makes short books more acceptable.

There is nothing worse than reading a book that is mostly filler. Don't do it. Keep it bare bones. As soon as you discover the last line, stop. You are done.

Once again, I think putting yourself on a time limit will keep you to the story and only the story. So the book is short. But it is done. If you are really hell bent on writing a bigger book, you can do a series of three day challenges. Let's say you want to write about growing up. You can write one three day memoir about your life in grade school. Write a second three day book about high school. Do a third of your time in college. Put those three books together and you have something more substantial.

The important part is not overstay your welcome. Start at a run and go on into the end and then take a quick bow and get out of there.

Slide Thirteen
Step Six - Get Your Book Out There for the World to See
If your book just stays in a drawer or a hard drive, have you really written?

Okay. That is a little bit too much. But I have to ask. Why are you writing this book? Is it for you to get the ideas out? To exorcize some demons and find some truths in your history? That's a good reason.

But then there are some of us so brazen to think that our words are not only good enough to be put into a book, but that other people should read it. We are a mad and unruly lot and we cannot be denied.

So I encourage you to do something with the book you wrote. Submit it to contests or editors. Try to get it published in the traditional way. Do it. There are a lot of books and classes that teach you to do it.

But we live in a crazy time where we can put the books out ourselves in a pretty easy manner. With Kindle and Kobo and Apple Books, you can upload your book to them in a manner of minutes. Like I said earlier, one of my books took just eight days from the initial idea to when it was available as an eBook. Through Kindle, you can also get a book version sold through print on demand.

Now there are downsides. It is really hard to get your book seen. Once again, you can read or take some classes on how to get your work discovered.

I have also gone through the process of getting some of these three day memoirs published as actual zines. The cost is quite reasonable. But then comes the annoying part of getting them into local bookstores. It is a drag, but man, it is worth it.

I love getting my books or Gwyn's book out there and have people hold it in their hands. Gwyn's book is incredibly brave and I am happy to have helped get it out in the world.

If you have a story to tell, then you need an audience. So don't just sit on the book, get it out there. Technology has allowed you to do it pretty easily.

I'm not saying any of this easy or not nerve wracking. It is. But it is so wonderful to put your work out. There is a lot more that you will need to learn how to do. You have to get it copyedited. You have to write ad copy. You have to make a cover for it. You can do it yourself or you can hire someone. Take the time and learn about this. There are great people who can teach you. What I can teach you is that you can write a small, but effective book in just three days.

There are too many people saying, "I have a story, but I don't know what to do with it." Well, finish it. Publish it. Write the next story.

Slide 14

You Have Permission

In the quote I read from Gwyn Campbell, she said that she wanted to write this personal history for some time, but felt that no one would want a 21 year old to write a book. She needed me asking her to write something to finally give permission.

How many amazing books have not been written because someone thinks that they don't have the right to create it?

Well, you have permission. You should do it. Make yourself a list of things you want to cover in your little book. Take some nice long walks to think about it further. Block off three days, or even three evenings, and then go and write it. If you don't finish it in time, then take a few more days to get it done. Get it out in front of people's eyes.

Let me know how it goes. Make your own zine where you can put out your memoirs. Or gang up with someone else and do it together.

I'm not going to publish the Long Weekend Review anymore; I am ending it. So, I cannot publish your book. But you don't need me. You can do it.

Slide 15

The End of The Long Weekend Review

Has publishing the zine filled with Three Day Memoirs made me financially successful? Not one bit. I do get money, but because I insist on charging only a dollar for the eBook, my royalties are very low. It's literally pennies. But I wanted to keep it low. I believe in cheap books for all. The other writers who did this project with me also were aware that the financial reward was minimal. But we got to write our books and get them out there. That works for me.

So why am I ending the zine? Because after a while, I was not getting other people writing three day books. So it was turning into me just writing another book every month. I have been able to keep up the schedule, while writing other things. But I feel that I don't want the zine to just be my voice every month.

I am worried that all I am is the guy who is writing memoir after memoir. At a poetry open mic, I thought I would read from my Rocky Horror memoir. The bartender at the place we run it scoffed. He said, the last thing we want is someone reading their little memoir story in a bar. He had a point. But, then, I still read from the book. I scoff at good advice.

If all I am writing is me-me-me all the time, even I will want to shut me up. Now, I am still going to write three day memoirs. I like doing it. I have two or three ideas I want to try in that challenge format. But I don't need to do it monthly.

This whole project of the three day book and the zine was formed through the stress of Covid. The first issue was all about what we were going through. This has kept my mind busy. Now, it has been exactly one full year since I started this. Covid is slowly ending, thank God. I and many others have already been vaccinated. It seems fitting that this whole project was a product of the pandemic. Now that it is ending, this is a good time to stop.

I also just want to try other things. I like doing a monthly eZine, but maybe I want to try some other format. I don't want to be stuck in one mode. One form.

And besides, I want to leave the stage, and give you all a chance to try it. The spotlight is yours.

But should I just leave without one last hoorah? One last three day memoir? Of course not. I have written a final one.

It's the one you are listening to now.

I take a pause, waiting for gasps of surprise. I don't get any. Oh well.

Slide 16
What You Have Listened to Is the Last Issue.
You Listened to Final Three Day Memoir

What you have been listening to is word for word what is in the final issue of The Long Weekend Review. I made sure that I read this word for word. I am pretty clever. Copies of it are for sale in the lobby in just a few minutes. Buy a few copies. For the kids.

And this was written in 71 hours. It pretty much went to the wire. But I did the math and it only took around nine hours of actual writing. I went for walks. Today, I even went to work. I wrote forty minutes in the morning and now, while dinner is bubbling in pots, I am finishing this thing up. I'm pretty good at writing quickly at this point, but you should be able to get a ten thousand word memoir done in three days.

And that's it. That's all you have to do. Find the time. Find a topic. Write quick.

You will be amazed by what you discover in the pages you type. Maybe some truth. Maybe something funny. Maybe a little bit of both.

I wish I had more tricks to give to you, but really, the best way to learn how to do it, is just get down to writing.

Please, pick up a copy of this book before leave. And forgive all the typos. I'm an adequate writer and a lousy copy editor. Good night.

And for the first time in an hour. I breathe. I feel weak. I talked fast and long. Some people come up and ask me if they should try to write a memoir. I say, "Yep." Some say they don't have the time, but they can give me an idea and I can write it for them. I beg off. I want to see what they can do. I already know what I have up my sleeve. Those people leave slightly annoyed.

Soon enough, everyone leaves. Off to their own books. Off to their own beds. I am alone in the big room.

Alright. Another book done. I wonder what I am going to write tomorrow. It's okay. I'll think of something.

Completed on March 15th, 2021 at 4:50 PM

About This Book

What can you write a memoir in three days?

David Macpherson wrote a memoir in three days. He liked it so much, he did it five more times. What you have in this book are the six small memoirs he wrote in three days a piece.

You will learn about the ins and outs of being a Rocky Horror kid. Or you experience a youth remembered in reference to the TV shows he watched. How about a small memoir about reading books while walking the dog? That's there too.

David wrote of the difficulty of being a young special needs teacher working with aggressive students. There is one about watching flicks at a movie theater during the Covid Pandemic. And finally, David created a memoir/manual about how to write a memoir in three days.

All different topics, all just one person. Written with honesty, humor and warmth, these little glimpses at person can let you see the whole. Pick up a copy because looking at small details can tell a large story.

About the Writer

Hi, it's David. Hope you are well. I am happy that you made it to this, the most important, part of the book. I am a writer from Central Massachusetts and have run poetry readings in Worcester for over a decade. I have put out around 60 eBooks. They are all over the map, you should check them out. I have written another brief memoir that I did not include in this volume, <u>I Kind of Knew Edward Gorey.</u> There are a lot of good books out there, have fun discovering new titles and writers.